**This may be one of the most impor... ...... you can read for improving your company's performance**

**Sales** & **Operations Planning** has emerged as an essential set of management tools in this age of global operations, supply chains that extend half a world away, and increasingly demanding customers. Its primary component – Executive S&OP – has rightfully been called "top management's handle on the business."

The mission of this book is to tell the busy executive what he or she needs to know about Executive S&OP. Written in clear, understandable language, this book can easily be read in the course of an evening or two – or on a plane ride from Chicago to L.A.

**It answers these, and many other, questions:**

.. Why is Executive S&OP so popular?

.. What are the benefits from doing it well?

.. How does it work?

.. What's the role of the president and his or her staff?

.. What kinds of companies are using Executive S&OP?

.. What's the best way to implement it?

**Tom Wallace** is a writer and educator specializing in sales & operations planning, sales forecasting, and demand management. Tom is a distinguished fellow of The Ohio State University's Center for Operational Excellence, and currently writes and speaks in conjunction with the Institute of Business Forecasting. He is the author of twelve books, including Sales & Operations Planning: The How-To Handbook.

**Bob Stahl** has spent the last 45+ years as a practitioner and consultant developing leading edge processes for manufacturing, logistics, and supply chain management. He is a teacher, writer, and consultant with an extremely strong track record of success. Bob has worked with many of the world's leading corporations and is the co-author of Building to Customer Demand, Sales Forecasting: A New Approach, Sales & Operations Planning: The Self-Audit Workbook, and Master Scheduling in the 21st Century.

For more information on the Tom Wallace or Bob Stahl, visit us at:

www.RAStahlCompany.com

# SALES & OPERATIONS PLANNING

## *Beyond the Basics*

# Also by Tom Wallace

## Books (co-authored with Bob Stahl):

*Sales & Operations Planning: The How-To Handbook, 3rd Ed.*

*Sales & Operations Planning: The Executive's Guide*

*Sales & Operations Planning: The Self-Audit Workbook, 2nd Ed.*

*Building to Customer Demand*

*Sales Forecasting: A New Approach*

*Master Scheduling in the 21st Century*

## Videos:

*The Executive S&OP Briefing: A Visual Introduction for Executives and Managers*

*The Education Kit for Sales & Operations Planning*

# Sales & Operations Planning
# Beyond the Basics

How Leading Companies Enhance and Extend

the Power of Executive S&OP

Thomas F. Wallace

T. F. Wallace & Company
2011

Third Edition
First Printing: March, 2008
Second Printing: April, 2008: Minor text corrections
Third Printing: January, 2009: Minor text corrections
Fourth Printing: July, 2010: Minor text corrections
Fifth Printing: June, 2015: Adding Steelwedge
Sixth Printing: May, 2016


Kindle Copy August 2018

International Standard Book Number: 978-0-9978877-0-9



Printed in the United States of America


Books and videos by Tom Wallace and/or Bob Stahl may be ordered online from:
www.RAStahlCompany.com.
Contact information:    R.A. Stahl Company

                        RStahlSr@aol.com
                        www.RAStahlCompany.com

# Contents

# Dedication

## to

## Richard A. Clark

## 1953 - 2011

Dick Clark, Associate Director of Global Network Supply Operations at Procter & Gamble, died shortly before this book went to press,

Dick was a fine man and a leader in the field of Sales & Operations Planning. Back in the mid-1990s, I taught S&OP to Dick and others from his company; it's gratifying to me that they have make such enormous progress with it, far beyond the basics I taught them fifteen years ago.

You'll hear from Dick in Chapter 12 of this book, the P&G case study. He was highly helpful to me in developing that chapter and also in reviewing the entire book.

Thanks, Dick. You will be missed.

# A Word About Terminology

The term Sales & Operations Planning traditionally referred to a decision-making process for balancing demand and supply in *aggregate.* This is a function that requires executive input and decision making.

However, common usage of this term has morphed — it's broadened to include tools and techniques that operate at a lower, more *detailed* level, for individual products and customer orders. These are hardly ever executive-centered processes; they carry too much detail.

To refer to the aggregate, executive-focused process, I'll use two terms: *Executive S&OP* and *S&OP.* To reflect the morphing that has occurred, the term *Sales & Operations Planning* will be used only for the larger set of processes, which include detailed activities as well as aggregate.

For more on this, see Appendix A: The Great Terminology Brouhaha.

# Acknowledgments

This book owes much of its existence to the group of people who provided the bulk of the information for these cases. Their efforts were extremely impressive, particularly when one considers that they all have full-time jobs plus. Furthermore, much of the work on this book took place during and after the Japanese earthquake and tsunami; some of the contributors are involved with outsourced products and components from Asia and thus were extraordinarily busy. But they managed to make time for their part in this book.

I think of these users as the *S&OP Experts*, and that's how I'll refer to them in this book. We don't have S&OP black belts or S&OP "senseis," and it's likely we never will. That's fine, because the term *S&OP Experts* will serve us well.

Here are the Experts, in alphabetical order by last name:

Dick Clark, Procter & Gamble

Kristoffer Lutz, Staples

Brad McCollum, Jarden

Alan Milliken, BASF

Sean Schubert, Newell Rubbermaid

Adam Szczepanski, formerly V&M Star

Melissa Takas, V&M Star

Brad Tallman, Cisco Systems

Scott Winstead, Dow Chemical

Shelly Zafrir, Applied Materials

To each and every one of these S&OP Experts, please accept a heartfelt "thanks a million" from yours truly and also, I hope, from the readers of this book. You have helped to move the ball down the field.

## A THANK YOU TO THE COMPANIES

All of us, the readers and this author, owe a substantial thank you to the participating companies. Agreeing to share information about a process that's vital to the company can be difficult, in certain cases impossible; some of the companies I asked to participate in this book declined for policy reasons based on privacy. Fortunately, I was able to recruit other companies to fill the gaps and the book has not suffered. This factor makes the contributions of the participating companies all the more significant. I thank you, and I trust the readers do also.

## AND IN ADDITION

I owe a "tip o' the hat" to Kim Nir — copy edit, David Mill — jacket design, and last, and most assuredly not least, to Kathryn Wallace and Amy McDuffie — page layout.

Kim, who lives in New Jersey, gets a special "thank you"; she had to copy edit the manuscript for this book at the same time she was coping with Tropical Storm Lee dumping enormous amounts of water on her home.

Thank you, folks — you do very good work.

# Foreword by Bob Stahl

Tom Wallace has been the leading writer of S&OP books for a long time, and it's been my pleasure to partner with him for the past ten years or so. Never has his work been more important than now, as the power of S&OP is expanding so quickly. This book chronicles some of what is taking place today, but S&OP will not stay static. Five or ten years from now, we might be amazed at how far we've come. Stay tuned.

Five or ten years ago, this book could not have been written; there simply weren't enough companies developing and using the kinds of advanced S&OP-based processes that are the focus here. This book describes the growing power of Executive S&OP, focusing on some of the many companies doing superb things with it.

How'd this happen? Well, several factors played into it but one group stands head and shoulders above the rest: they're the users, the people in companies. They're the ones who connected the dots — one dot being Executive S&OP and their knowledge of it and the other dot being business problems their companies were experiencing. The practitioners — deservedly called *S&OP Experts* in this book — are the ones who truly moved the ball down the field, and who will continue to do so.

When S&OP was first developed, it did some very good things, but at that early stage of the game, I didn't fully appreciate its power, its potential, or what it would evolve into as the decades unfolded. No one did. Certainly not my colleagues, nor the early users.

This book drives a stake in the ground. It describes a view of the S&OP state-of-the-art in 2011. It directly refutes the words of the naysayers, such as: "This stuff won't work," "It's merely an old process wrapped in a new name," "It won't fit this or that business," and so on.

Enough! We've heard those comments much too often. That's over. S&OP is real; it's valid; it's here to stay; and it will continue to get better. To those of you who are not yet using it, I say disregard it at your peril. To those of you already using it, I say improve it, make it more powerful and more useful to your company. You've got some great teachers right here in this book: the S&OP Experts.

Bob Stahl
Plymouth, Massachusetts

# Chapter 1

# Building the Foundation

A disclaimer: Some people may think Tom Wallace invented Sales & Operations Planning. I did not . . . but I was present at its birth. My colleague Dick Ling comes closest to being the inventor; during the early 1980s, Dick and I were members of the Oliver Wight organization and both of us served on its management committee. I cheered Dick's efforts from the sidelines.

We were enthused about this new process. We saw S&OP as a superior way to do two highly important things:

- **to balance demand and supply**, and to keep them balanced over time as demand and other factors shift

- **to integrate operational plans with financial plans**, enabling the business to be run internally with one set of numbers.

These are solutions to problems afflicting companies forever: demand and supply not in balance and multiple sets of numbers that don't agree. The early users — the ones who did it successfully — were equally enthused. And so the word started to get around: *Here's a process that has a great deal of power, requires relatively few people, does not require new software, and can be implemented quickly.*

More companies tried it, some quite successfully and some not so much. But, as with virtually every new process of this type, the early adoption rate was low.[1] Gradually, however, more and more companies tried it and did it well. The base of successful S&OP users was expanding. However, back then, no one really had an idea how powerful this process could become. We knew it was good, but we were far from knowing how good it could be. Now we know.

Other positive things started to happen in companies doing S&OP well: They found that they could build new capabilities into their

---

[1] For more on this, see Appendix B: Coming Up the Adoption Curve.

S&OP processes beyond the basic ones of balancing demand and supply and integrating operational and financial planning.

These new developments did not go unreported. One would hear about them in conferences, and read about them in magazines and e-mails. Unfortunately, there was no common repository for this information, not any one place where people could look to see the many good things taking place. S&OP was becoming more and more powerful, better able to support companies in meeting their specific problems and opportunities — but this information wasn't as available as it should have been.

That's why I wrote this book. It's intended to present advanced practices, in use today, that build on the basic S&OP processes of demand/supply balance and operational/financial integration.

Another disclaimer: It is not intended to be a compilation of *all or even most* of the S&OP-based advanced practices in use today. That would be impossible: I don't know them all; it would take forever to write; and by the time it was completed, there would be a whole new bunch of recently-developed advanced practices that should be included. The book would never get finished.

As you read some of the cases, you may find yourself wishing for more specifics on how they do a certain thing. However, this is not a "how-to" book. Don't expect to read it and learn the nitty-gritty of how Company A enhanced its Executive S&OP processes and was able to do great things. There are no formulas here, and not many detailed flow charts or intricate process diagrams.

This book is intended to be an "idea generator," a "consciousness raiser." You will see the big pictures that show what some companies did to enhance their processes and thereby accomplish superb results.

It's meant to get you thinking about how some of these advanced processes could help your company, done somewhat differently no doubt because your company is not the same as those in this book; your environment, ownership, customer base — and your goals — are probably quite different.

## THE MISSION OF EXECUTIVE S&OP

Executive S&OP needs to add new capabilities as the business environment evolves. I won't be giving you a lot of blue sky, theory, if-come-maybe, or whatever. Everything presented here will be based on what leading-edge users of the process are doing to help themselves run their businesses better.

A word about these users is in order. As Bob Stahl indicates in the Foreword, true progress in this field is not made by consultants, coaches, software vendors, academics, or authors (ouch). Their role is to communicate and disseminate, and also, on occasion, to assist the users. But true progress is made by the users, the people running businesses and building increasingly powerful processes. That's why we think of them as experts.

Executive S&OP, in its basic form, helps people to balance demand and supply at an aggregated, volume level and to integrate operational planning with financial planning. That's pretty much what it was when it got started around 1980.

We need to get a baseline understanding of the fundamentals of Executive S&OP. Then, throughout this book, we'll use this understanding as a foundation to learn how leading-edge companies are building on the basics, and going beyond them, to make the process even more powerful and more beneficial.

## EIGHT ELEMENTARY ERRORS

First, we'll tackle the issue of what S&OP is not. These are the myths, misconceptions, and misunderstandings that get in the way of people comprehending that S&OP is a superb tool — one that can benefit their company greatly. Here goes:

**#1** *We don't need S&OP in our department; that's a "supply chain thing."*

Reality: Yes, it is a supply chain thing — and a sales & marketing thing — and a manufacturing thing — and a finance thing — and an R&D thing — and, last but not least, it's a *top management* thing. Executive S&OP is a company-wide, collaborative decision-making process, reaching to the top levels in the business.

**#2** *We'll never get S&OP to work — we don't have enough teamwork.*

Reality: You've got it backwards. Executive S&OP doesn't require teamwork before you get started; it *engenders* teamwork once it's operating properly. It enables people to view the business holistically and thus see their colleagues' problems. A company that is implementing Executive S&OP but is not getting improved teamwork means just one thing: They didn't do it right.

**#3** *S&OP is too rigid. It won't work for us because our business changes too quickly.*

Reality: Executive S&OP is all about change. It provides a "window into the future," so that companies can: 1) see problems months ahead of time, 2) take corrective action, and 3) prevent potential problems from becoming real ones. S&OP is, among other things, a coordination tool, and coordination is needed most when things are changing.

**#4** *We can't use S&OP because we don't have any manufacturing. We use contract manufacturers exclusively.*

Reality: Executive S&OP doesn't care who owns the factory. Actually, companies that outsource heavily probably need it more, because they will generally have less control over the supply side of their businesses. We also see S&OP being used in banks, retail companies, engineering organizations, and IT.

5 *We're a large company. I think we're too big for S&OP.*

Reality: Are you bigger than Procter & Gamble, for example? Or bigger than BASF, the world's largest chemical company? We see these companies, and a growing number of others, using Executive S&OP very successfully in their operating business units. Furthermore, in some of these companies, the results from the operating units' S&OP processes are rolled up, communicated to the corporate CEO, and form a key component of the corporation's earnings calls to Wall Street.

#6 *We have to get our forecasts a lot better before we think about S&OP.*

Reality: Here also, you've got it backwards. Almost always, implementing Executive S&OP helps to improve the forecasts. One reason is, for the first time, people start to view forecasting as a *process* rather than a pain in the neck. They see that it plays a vital role in the overall S&OP process and hence how well the business is run. Thus they view it as much more important than before.

If you wait for your forecasts to improve before you tackle S&OP, you may wait a long time.

#7 *We don't need S&OP; we're doing Lean Manufacturing.*

Reality: Executive S&OP and Lean are two very different things. S&OP is a medium-to-long-term planning tool that provides visibility into the future, thereby avoiding surprises when demand shifts — up or down. People who know both S&OP and Lean say, "They work best when they work together."

#8 *S&OP is really simple. We're just going to get the spreadsheets working and then we'll have S&OP.*

Reality: Yes, S&OP is simple if you're talking about the internal logic of the process. Of much greater significance are the mindsets of the people — all the way up to the president — who will use it.

Implementing Executive S&OP successfully is largely a matter of change management, requiring cultural change for the organization and behavioral change by individuals. It's people intensive, and that's where the emphasis needs to be during an implementation.

## REALITIES SUMMARIZED

Now let's eliminate the noise coming from those myths, and focus on the good news:

- Executive S&OP is a company-wide, multi-level, collaborative decision-making process, reaching to the top levels in the business.

- S&OP engenders teamwork because it provides a holistic view of the business.

- As such, it aligns human energy, helping people to move in the same direction, and enables them to better control their own collective destiny.

- S&OP provides a "window into the future" so that companies can better prevent potential problems from becoming real ones.

- S&OP doesn't care who owns the factory: the company itself, or its contract manufacturers, toll producers, outsource suppliers, and so forth.

- S&OP enables much stronger alignment and collaboration with Finance and financial plans, made possible by being able to run the business internally with one set of numbers.

- S&OP can provide major assistance in making quarterly earnings calls.

- Almost always, implementing S&OP helps to improve the forecasts.

- People who know both S&OP and Lean Manufacturing say, "They work best when they work together."

- Implementing Executive S&OP successfully is largely a matter of change management.

## THE MONTHLY EXECUTIVE S&OP PROCESS

The essence of Executive S&OP is decision making. For each product family, a decision is made on the basis of recent history, recommendations from middle management, and the executive team's knowledge of business conditions. The decision can be:

1. change the Sales Plan,

2. change the Operations Plan,

3. change the projected finished inventory or customer order backlog, or

4. none of the above: The current plans are okay.

These decisions form the agreed-upon, authorized plans by the president, all involved vice presidents, and other members of the executive group. They form the overall game plan for Sales, Operations, Finance, and Product Development. (New product plans are reviewed within Executive S&OP for their needs and their impact on the demand and supply picture.)

Executive S&OP, however, is not a single event that occurs in a one-to-two-hour Executive meeting each month. Rather, preliminary work begins shortly after month's end and continues for some days. The steps involve middle management and others throughout the company (see Figure 1-1). They include:

- updating the Sales Forecast — the Demand Plan;

- reviewing the impact of changes on the Operations Plan — the Supply Plan — and determining whether adequate capacity and material will be available to support them;

- identifying alternatives where problems exist;

- identifying variances to the Business Plan (budget) and potential solutions;

- formulating agreed-upon recommendations for top management regarding overall changes to the plans, identifying areas of disagreement where consensus is not possible, and then communicating this information to top management with sufficient time for them to review it prior to the Executive meeting.

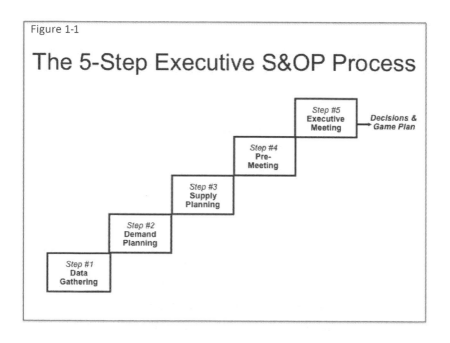

Figure 1-1

# The 5-Step Executive S&OP Process

Thanks to the work that's gone before, the monthly Executive meeting should not take a long time — one to two hours is the norm with companies that do this well. The net result of Executive S&OP for the top management group should be less time in meetings, more productivity in their decision-making processes, enhanced teamwork, and a higher quality of work life. And most of the middle-management and other people involved in the earlier processes — from areas such as Demand Planning, Supply Planning, Finance, and New Products — will experience the same benefits.

Throughout this book, we'll be looking at companies that are enhancing their Executive S&OP processes to stay in sync with their businesses as they grow. I believe that S&OP must grow in capability as businesses become increasingly complex, in order to support the people using it. That's its job.

Let's close this chapter with some words from Andrew Downard, Director of Supply Chain at Newell Rubbermaid, a diversified consumer products company and a very successful user of Executive S&OP.

*S&OP really lies at the heart of the business. The moment you touch it, the ripples start spreading everywhere — demand planning, business forecasting, capacity management, supply planning, budgeting, business reviews, organizational structures, you name it.*

*In some cases, like demand planning and forecasting, we saw immediate benefits from improving S&OP. In other cases, like inventory optimization, S&OP has provided a solid foundation, but we still have plenty of work to do. We had to start somewhere, and having a strong S&OP process provides a great foundation to improve all of the other processes it touches.*

Spot on! Andrew's closing words — *"a great foundation to improve all of the other processes it touches"* — strike me as capturing the essence of this book.

# Chapter 2

# Company Cases and the Experts

This book centers on a handful of advanced S&OP topics:

Strategy Enhancement

Advanced Financial Planning

Risk Management

Global S&OP

Advanced Demand Planning

Advanced Supply Planning

New Product Launch

Process Metrics

Non-Standard Applications

Tied to each topic are one or several company cases. In some situations, one case supports multiple topics; for example the BASF case has relevance to Strategy Enhancement, Advanced Supply Planning, and Global S&OP.

## THE COMPANIES

**Applied Materials, Inc**. — a capital equipment manufacturer based in Santa Clara, California serving the semiconductor and other manufacturing industries. Annual revenue: $9.5 billion US (2010). This case focuses on Applied's business unit in Israel. S&OP Expert for this book: Shelly Zafrir, Director of Sales & Operations Planning in Santa Clara.

**BASF** — the largest chemical company in the world, headquartered in Ludwigshafen, Germany and doing business extensively on a global basis. Annual revenue: €63.9 billion (2010). S&OP Expert for this book: Alan Milliken, Business Process Education Manager, North America.

**Cisco Systems, Inc.** — designs and sells consumer electronics, networking, voice, and communications technology and services. Based in San Jose, California., it has annual revenue: $40.0 billion US (2010). S&OP Expert for this book: Brad Tallman, Senior Director, Sales & Operations Planning.

**Dow Chemical Company** — headquartered in Midland, Michigan, is a provider of plastics, chemicals, and agricultural products, and heavily engaged in business worldwide. Annual revenue: $53.6 US (2010). S&OP Expert for this book: Scott Winstead, Supply Chain Improvement Director for a major Dow business.

**Jarden Corporation** — headquartered in Rye, New York, is a provider of consumer products used in and around the home. It has over 20,000 employees worldwide. Annual revenue: $6.0 billion (FY 2010). S&OP Expert for this book: Brad McCollum, Manager of Sales & Operations Planning, Jarden Leisure and Entertainment Group.

**Newell Rubbermaid** — supplies an extensive variety of business and consumer products. It is headquartered near Atlanta, Georgia. Annual revenue: $5.8 billion US (FY 2010). S&OP Expert for this book: Sean Schubert, Senior Manager, Supply Chain.

**Procter & Gamble** — headquartered in Cincinnati, Ohio and one of the world's largest producers of consumer products. It ranked fifth in Fortune Magazine's Most Admired Companies list in 2011. Annual revenue: $78.9 billion (FY 2010). S&OP Expert for this book: Dick Clark, Associate Director, Demand Planning and Global Process Leader and coach for the S&OP process.

**Staples, Inc.** — based in Framingham, Massachusetts. Specializing in office products, its revenue in 2010 was $24.5 billion. This case will focus on Staples' North American Delivery business. S&OP Expert for this book: Kristoffer Lutz, Director of Sales & Operations Planning.

**V&M Star** — a component of Vallourec & Mannesman Tubes, headquartered in France and the world market leader in the manufacture of seamless hot rolled steel tubes. This unit, based in Houston, Texas, was formerly part of North Star Steel. S&OP Experts are Melissa Takas, Operations Controlling Supervisor and Adam Szczepanski, formerly Chief Financial Officer.

Now let's look at the relationship among the topics and the cases.

| Topic | Company | Chapter |
|---|---|---|
| Strategy Enhancement | BASF | 3 |
| | Cisco Systems | 4 |
| | Dow Chemical | 5 |
| Financial Planning | V&M Star | 6 |
| | Procter & Gamble | 12 |
| Risk Management | Jarden | 9 |
| Global S&OP | BASF | 3 |
| | Procter & Gamble | 12 |
| Demand Planning | Cisco Systems | 4 |
| | Applied Materials | 8 |
| Supply Planning | Jarden | 9 |
| | BASF | 3 |
| New Product Launch | Jarden | 9 |
| | Newell Rubbermaid | 7 |
| Process Metrics | Procter & Gamble | 12 |
| Non-Standard Applications | Staples | 11 |

So now it's time to take a look, starting with BASF.

# Chapter 3

# Company: BASF

**Areas of Focus:** **1. Enhancing Business Strategy**
**2. Global S&OP**
**3. Advanced Supply Planning**

Author's comments: One of the most surprising aspects of Executive S&OP is the profound effect it can have on a business. Over the years, I've repeatedly been struck by what companies accomplish by using this tool intelligently. And it doesn't seem to matter whether they're small, medium, or large businesses — or which industry they're in.

Our first case is BASF, a large and very successful chemical company. Let's look at S&OP's role in helping them achieve that size and success.

## OPTIMIZING PROFIT VIA GLOBAL S&OP

BASF
Ludwigshafen am Rhein, Germany
Products: Chemicals
Annual Sales: €63.9 billion

BASF is the world's largest producer of chemical products, billing itself simply as "The Chemical Company." With more than 100,000 employees, this 150-year old company does business globally, utilizing about 100 large sites and many smaller ones.

BASF wasn't always the largest player in the chemical industry, experiencing substantial growth over the last decade and bypassing major competitors to become number one. Alan Milliken, Business Process Education Manager for BASF, who has deep experience in S&OP, says "*While BASF does many things well, S&OP has contributed significantly to helping us achieve our present position in the industry.*"

BASF operates in 80 countries around the world, and is divided into more than 60 strategic business units primarily along product lines. The nature of the chemical business is such that plants are often highly product-specific, almost from the ground up; as such, a given plant will often "belong" to the business that markets the product. This results in a multiplicity of business units, each one of which will have its own Executive S&OP process with the goal of operating S&OP globally to leverage synergies and maximize profitability.

We'll look at an example from a typical BASF business and keep in mind this is only one of the many different operating units within BASF cited above, some with annual sales well into the billions of euros. This business has five plants, located Europe, China, Korea, the United States, and a joint venture in Japan.

The plants do not "belong" to any region; rather they produce product for more than one region, in some cases all of them. Furthermore, at some of these plants, a majority of the volume goes outside the region where the plant is located. So the challenge is to capture demand from each of the four regions and assign the related production volumes to the plants on an *optimal "best fit" basis.* The overall goal is to maximize operating results (profits) within the desired service level and inventory targets.

## THE PROCESS

BASF's Global Executive S&OP process is shown in Figure 3-1. We can see some interesting departures from the standard seven-step global process:[1]

- The demand plan is done on a regional basis, the reason being that the regions are closest to the customer and are held accountable for attaining the sales volume in their forecast.

- These plans are then consolidated into a global picture of demand.

---

[1] For more on this, see *Sales & Operations Planning: The How-To Handbook, Third Edition*, by Wallace and Stahl, pp167–169.

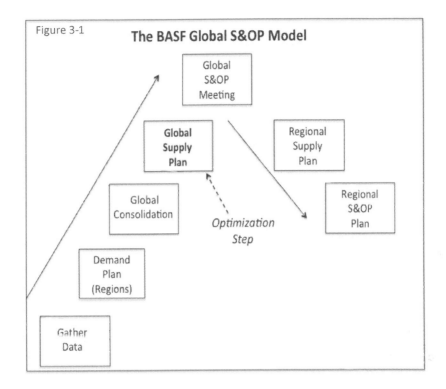

Figure 3-1

**The BASF Global S&OP Model**

- Supply is planned on a global rather than regional basis, for the reason cited above: the need to optimize the allocation of production. This is done quarterly by the Global Supply Chain Planner[2] using an advanced planning system (APS) software tool.

- With these two sets of plans, the business is ready to conduct its Global S&OP meeting. Prior to the Global S&OP Meeting, the Global Supply Chain Planner works with the regions and plants to identify and resolve issues with the preliminary plan. Only exceptions requiring executive-level input are elevated to the Global S&OP meeting, which normally takes place during the third week of the month.

[2] The Global Supply Chain Planner is a pivotal figure in this process. This function for a given business typically resides in either Europe or the United States and serves as the primary coordination point for most S&OP issues.

In many of the BASF business units, this process is done monthly, and our sample business does it that way. However, some operate on a quarterly basis, depending on a variety of factors: the business strategy, the complexity of the network, the size of the business unit, lead times, and others. For example, a business producing commodity products is primarily driven by cost, not flexibility, as it has little control over prices, which are set by the marketplace. A stable plan for more than one month at a time may be a real asset to this business in maximizing efficiency in the plants. Figure 3-2 shows inputs, constraints, and outputs for the Optimization Run.

---

Figure 3-2

### S&OP Optimization Run:
### Maximize Gross Profits Globally

**Key Inputs:**
- Current Prices
- Total Delivered Cost (source to customer)
- Demand Forecasts
- Production Capabilities
- Inventory Levels

**Key Constraints:**
- Inventory Targets
- Load-Dependent Plant Costs (minimum loads identified)
- Customer Service Level Targets (must be met)

**Key Outputs:**
- Production Plan by Product Family/Plant
- Gross Operating Profit Based on S&OP Plan

### Results: A Production Plan Optimized
### Globally on Gross Profit

---

The Global Supply Chain Planner is responsible for identifying issues within the re-planning cycle and working with the S&OP team to resolve those issues. Pre-established rules are used to control the change process and ensure total economics are the driving force.

## BENEFITS

Alan Milliken reported the following benefits being realized from the global approach:

- Shift from an emphasis on local volume one of to *global value*. Instead of each region focusing on maximizing their utilization rates and thus minimizing their cost, the focus is on global profitability.

- Increased visibility across the supply chain (Inventories, Sales, etc.). All S&OP participants have access to demand, supply, and inventory data in the system.

- Global transparency of supply chain costs and focus on total delivered cost. All regions review and the optimal solution and provide qualitative inputs before the plan is finalized.

- Improved communications and teamwork across regions and functions. Both the plan and the Key Performance Indicators (KPIs) are global, which encourages interaction between the regions and functions.

- Last and definitely not least, increased profitability through simulation and optimization. The software can perform "what if?" scenarios for review by the S&OP team and will optimize gross margins based on pre-established objectives and logic.

Here's Alan again: *"S&OP, because of the way we use it to optimize production, has had a significant impact on the bottom line. So much so that BASF's global leadership has recognized the importance of S&OP by activating a permanent team of Global S&OP Process Experts to ensure harmonization on best practices and continuous improvement of the process."*

\*     \*     \*     \*     \*

The moral of the story: Alan's earlier statement — S&OP has played a substantial role in BASF's move into first place worldwide in the chemical business — illustrates the enormous power of this process. This is an excellent example of using S&OP to help achieve big, "hairy" strategic goals: in this case, becoming Number One in their industry.

People sometimes ask: "Is Executive S&OP a strategic tool or a tactical tool?" My first answer, tongue in cheek, is "yes." Now for the real answer: It is not a strategic tool in the narrow sense of the word. It doesn't help to set the strategy for the organization. However, as we've just seen, it enhances the company's ability to achieve its strategies. That's what happened with BASF and also in our next two cases.

There is a relationship between the strategic/tactical issue and the time frame. In the short term, S&OP is almost totally tactical; medium term, it becomes somewhat more strategic; long term, it's focused heavily on strategic issues. — TW

# Chapter 4

# Company: Cisco Systems

**Areas of Focus:**   **1. Enhancing Business Strategy**
**2. New Product Launch**

Author's comments: People sometimes ask me: Tom, we make widgets. Would S&OP work in the widget industry?

Well, S&OP has amazingly wide application potential. We've just seen its use in a chemical manufacturer; now we'll look at a high-tech company involved in a complex new product launch somewhat outside its comfort zone. In the Staples case (Chapter 11), we'll see a company that's not in manufacturing at all, but rather in online retail.

S&OP's ability to assist a company is quite independent of product, markets served, company size, internal processes, and so on.

---

## S&OP SUPPORT IN CREATING A NEW BUSINESS

Cisco Systems
San Jose, California
Products: Commercial and Consumer Electronics
Annual Sales: $40 billion (2010)

Cisco is the world leader in networking gear. Founded in 1985, it now has 300+ product families through these business segments: Commercial, Enterprise, Service Provider, Small, and Public Sector. It does business in 165 countries throughout five theaters (regions).

### EXECUTIVE S&OP AT CISCO

S&OP has come a long way at Cisco in a relatively few years. The company was hit hard in the early 2000s, when the tech bubble burst and Cisco was left with large amounts of excess and obsolete inventory; this event plus other factors have led the company to sharply improve its S&OP processes.

This task has been made tougher by the complex nature of the businesses, Cisco having acquired over 140 other companies — some of which are larger than $1 billion in annual sales — and a continued, rapid pace of acquisition.

Cisco today relies heavily on its excellent S&OP process to ensure that critical inputs, cadence, and engaged stakeholders are in place; this enables them to achieve consensus-based plans that are strategically aligned with business goals. This is not easy in an corporation of large size, rapid technology change, and a constantly changing organization due to the pace of acquisition mentioned previously.

The mission of Executive S&OP at Cisco is to provide the company with significant support in the following areas:

- **Visibility** — provide information on available supply and the potential upside

- **Velocity** — enable faster response to new market opportunities

- **Alignment** — help align key parts of the organization — Sales, Operations, Finance, Customer Value Chain Management (supply chain) and others — on a consensus shipment plan

- **Decision Making** — provide information to drive executive decisions on revenue and margin trade-offs

## CREATING A NEW PRODUCT AND A NEW BUSINESS

Here's an example of how Cisco's Executive S&OP process achieved its mission on a major, high-impact initiative.

In 2006, Cisco created a new business unit aimed at establishing leadership in an emerging video collaboration market known as *TelePresence*. One can think of it as "video conferencing on steroids."

TelePresence simulates a conference room, half of which I'll call Part A, consisting of six chairs around a table curved in a gentle arc, facing a large screen. The other half, Part B, is identical to the first except that it can be thousands of miles away. The people sitting in Part A see the Part B people on the screen, who appear to be sitting across the table, and vice versa for the Part B people. See Figure 4-1.

Figure 4-1        Cisco TelePresence System CTS 3000

The competitive landscape encompassed a handful of entrenched industry specialists with a not insignificant customer base, but far smaller than what Cisco felt it could generate. While future market acceptance of the Cisco TelePresence offering was largely unknown in terms of the duration of the sales cycle, volumes, and overall market share to be captured, the TelePresence Business Unit forecasted significant market share capture in the first six months after launch and recognized the possibility of "runaway scenarios."

The view from the supply side showed the following:

- The product line at launch consisted of two finished units, the CTS-1000 and the CTS-3000, the difference being mainly in the number of screens: one for the 1000 and three for the 3000.

- A complicating factor was the large number of new suppliers, some of whom supplied items far afield from Cisco's procurement experience and expertise, for example, wood for the half-moon conference tables.

- In Cisco's frame of reference, some of the component lead times were exceptionally lengthy: up to twice as long as its average component lead times.

- A somewhat different manufacturing model existed here, also outside of Cisco's experience, which traditionally involves contract manufacturers performing many pre-production steps as well as providing the finished product. Here Cisco was more deeply involved with multi-tiered production than in the past.

## EXECUTIVE S&OP'S ROLE

A monthly S&OP cycle was initiated with key TelePresence Business Unit leaders and the Cisco Value Chain Management (CVCM) support staff to review and set strategy against key operational objectives. Its initial purpose was to prepare Cisco for a wide range of potential demand scenarios involving rapid market growth. Topics addressed included:

- Demand-Supply Scenarios

- Inventory Buffering Strategies

- Product Supply Chain Strategies

- Product Quality Updates

- Upside Flexibility Targets

- International Contract Manufacturing Strategies

- Component Sourcing Strategies

- Capacity Expansion

- Order Management

- and more . . .

The S&OP players worked with the Marketing team to understand the high-low scenarios for first six months after launch and to address the one-to-two-year growth plan in terms of both product volumes and offerings. They engaged the cross-functional CVCM team to:

1. Ensure that development, operational planning, and execution were aligned to the agreed-on plan.

2. Identify critical long lead time components and build flexibility strategies around these key items.

3. Execute purchase orders based on recommendations regarding flexibility strategy from S&OP discussions with Business Unit executive management.

## IMPACT

So how did things work out? Did all this up-front hard work pay off? Let's take a look, first at the bad news.

### Negatives

The plan to buffer supply resulted in a short-term inventory build-up as early bookings were light. Bookings forecast accuracy in the first six months after launch was quite low to the negative side — a phenomenon not unusual with new product launches.

Increased overhead costs resulted from the large inventory build-up, which required additional warehouse space to manage the size and volume of the strategic buffer.

Inconsistent ordering by Cisco caused supplier concerns. This was triggered by major demand fluctuations month-to-month as Marketing aligned short-term growth aspirations with market realities and these changes were reflected in the schedules sent to the suppliers.

High rework costs were incurred on the accumulated inventory due to product enhancements often causing component changes, and also due to quality issues that emerged during the initial year.

## Positives

Now for the good news. First, there were no significant lead time increases due to component problems, neither during the launch period nor during the four + years that the product has been on the market (as of this writing.) This enabled rapid internal responsiveness and order management flexibility for key customer deployments, resulting in a current installed base, worldwide, of well over 1,000 units.

Despite the volatile shipment profiles, manufacturing lead times remained very stable: less than five days between order release and shipment. Further, the On-Time Shipment goal of >98% has consistently been met or exceeded. Customer complaints have been few and far between.

Last and certainly not least, Cisco now holds the number one market share position in this multi-billion dollar market.

Bryan Chase, Manager of Supply Chain Management, stated:

*Without S&OP, there's no way we could have generated the 98%+ on-time shipping performance and the rapid response between order and shipment. We feel very, very good about how well this initiative was planned and executed.*

Here's how Brad Tallman, Senior Director of Sales & Operations Planning, summed up his feelings about this initiative:

*We at Cisco consider the TelePresence story a great example of how S&OP can make major contributions to executing the company's strategy. Being an early mover into a new market requires a very different approach than when we take on more mature markets, regardless of our market position.*

*Would we have launched the TelePresence product without S&OP? Sure, but it would have taken longer; our inventory overstock problem would have been substantially greater; our relationships with contract manufacturers and component suppliers would have been far more at risk; and our customers would have had to bear the brunt of the uncertainty that comes with developing a new technology market.*

*At the end of the day, we knew that first-mover advantage in this space was critical for the business to gain traction and develop market leadership. Supporting this strategy in a profitable manner was our primary focus within S&OP.*

*   *   *   *   *

The moral of the story: My first point here concerns the introduction of new products. S&OP can play a major role in making new product launch quicker, more effective and, as Bob Stahl says, "more sure-footed." We see this time and again in many companies; Cisco's story here is no exception, except for the magnitude of the project.

Further, there has been positive spillover to other parts of the corporation. The complexities inherent in launching the TelePresence product have led to significant improvements in Cisco's forecasting and planning processes for new product introduction. Through better analytics and more robust market intelligence, Cisco has seen improvement in its ability to forecast within new markets and for new products.

Last, think of the contrast between our first two cases: BASF is almost 150 years old; Cisco is less than 30; BASF is in a mature market and headquartered in a mature part of the world; Cisco is in high-tech and located in what I call "that parallel universe in Silicon Valley." (It's different out there, folks.) We've seen that Executive S&OP has significantly supported both companies in achieving major strategic objectives — TW

# Chapter 5

# Company: Dow Chemical

## Area of Focus:    Enhancing Business Strategy

Author's comments: Dow Chemical is a long-term, successful user of S&OP. Their S&OP people are very knowledgeable about the process but my guess is that neither they nor I ever thought to use S&OP for the purpose described in this case. It's yet another example of the process being helpful in areas outside of its early charter of balancing demand and supply and integrating the financials.

---

## USING EXECUTIVE S&OP TO FACILITATE A MAJOR ACQUISITION

The Dow Chemical Company
Midland, Michigan
Products: Specialty and Basic Chemicals, Plastics
Annual Sales: $53.7 billion (2010)

Dow's acquisition of Rohm and Haas is part of Dow's long-term strategy of moving more heavily into specialty chemicals, which usually offer higher margins and greater growth potential. No doubt this transaction will be recognized as one of the more contentious in business history.

Why? Well, as an astute individual once said: "Timing is everything." The acquisition was initiated near the onset of The Great Recession; chemical sales declined; funding became difficult; attempts were made to delay the deal; legal actions were taken to make it happen. And the deal did happen; Dow acquired Rohm and Haas. Once that occurred, it fell to the people in the two corporations to pick up the pieces and learn to work together.

This involved blending business units from one company into another, perhaps a Dow business into a Rohm and Haas business, or the other way around, or perhaps both businesses into a brand new operating unit. The Dow businesses directly affected by the acquisition represented about 25% of the total, meaning that a quarter of Dow and most of Rohm and Haas's businesses would be impacted. No small challenge, particularly given the history of the acquisition; rather, it proved to be a change management task of enormous complexity — and importance. See Figure 5-1.

Figure 5-1

### Comparison: Dow Chemical – Rohm and Haas

Pre-Acquisition Data (year-end 2008)

|  | DOW CHEMICAL | ROHM and HAAS |
|---|---|---|
| Headquarters: | Midland, MI | Philadelphia, PA |
| Annual Sales: | $57.5 billion | $9.6 billion |
| # Employees : | 46,000 | 15,500 |
| # Key Bus. Units: | 17 | 10 |
| # Plants: | 150 | 98 |
| # Countries: | 175 | 27 |
| Primary products: |  |  |
| | Basic & specialty chemicals | Specialty chemicals |
| | Basic & specialty plastics | |
| | Agricultural products | |

In the supply chain planning part of the new Dow, the situation contained both good news and bad:

GOOD NEWS: Both companies were operating S&OP and recognized its value.

BAD NEWS: The two S&OPs were quite different, with different perceptions by the people as to what S&OP could do. Also, the two companies were drawing data from different enterprise software platforms.

GOOD NEWS: Achieving the worthwhile goal of having all business units use a common S&OP process around the world was established by senior management as a "must-do."

BAD NEWS: This meant that either Dow or Rohm and Haas (or both) would have to give up some elements of their S&OP processes.

BAD NEWS: In terms of enterprise software, Dow was running SAP R2 while Rohm and Haas was on SAP R3. A decision from the top said that there should be no attempt to merge operational systems until after Dow moved up to the next generation of software, some time into the future. Well, if this route of integration was not available, what process should be used to provide that integration, to be the glue that would join the new organizations together?

GOOD NEWS: S&OP took on this role. It became one of the key integrating processes, the glue that helped blend these disparate organizations into one.

## HOW IT HAPPENED

The total integration effort contained a key element: Functional Integration Teams (FIT), consisting of key players from both companies. Each function (Supply Chain, Manufacturing, Marketing and Sales, IT, etc.) had FITs established as part of the broader Rohm and Haas integration effort. In this way, each FIT could focus on its specific improvement efforts (cost synergy realization and others) as well as work together across functions to better coordinate efforts and improvements.

Within the Supply Chain FIT, there were two key sub-teams: Balance Demand & Supply (BDS) and Logistics. The BDS sub-team had responsibility for the various supply chain planning areas (S&OP, inventory replenishment, production planning/detailed scheduling, and so forth).

In order to make the BDS sub-team effective, there were key roles filled from each of the two companies to understand and identify key work processes, technologies, best practices, and potential improvement areas to realize cost synergies.

The Supply Chain FIT was given a "cost synergy target" of $75 million in cost savings resulting directly from the integration effort. This excludes cost savings from purchasing economies, plant and R&D lab closings, and so on. It also excludes revenue from increased business, even though in many acquired businesses, the increased revenue factor is substantial. Please note: These are not "funny numbers"; Dow prides itself on its history of hitting its cost synergy targets, citing its success in prior deals with Union Carbide, Angus Chemical, and others.

The BDS sub-team started to assess work processes within the two companies. It became clear that, for new businesses containing both Dow and Rohm and Haas elements, they would need to re-engineer their S&OP processes to get a common view of demand and supply, as well as to make decisions about imbalances. This was further complicated by having, as we said, two different ERP platforms that stored the demand and supply information.

The BDS sub-team decided to use a methodology called the "Dow S&OP Best Practice" as a way to improve and accelerate business-planning processes and deliver cost synergy savings. The Best Practice documentation contains a full implementation methodology including change management, detailed work processes, as well as specific roles and responsibilities. This is tied to a monthly S&OP process and S&OP technology to help collect, store, and analyze demand, supply, inventory, and performance metrics.

One of the important features of Dow's S&OP best practice is its focus on the principles of Executive S&OP. Here are several of the key principles that Dow has established:

1. Extend the planning horizon to 36 months to have businesses place more focus on strategic decision-making involving demand/ supply imbalances.

2. Decouple volume decision-making from that of mix and build work processes and technologies that reflect this, for example:

   • Focus on the 3-to-36-month horizon

   • Demand should be expressed in market families; supply in supply families

   • Decision-making centered in demand/supply imbalances

   • A clear financial view of imbalances and trade-offs, and so forth

3. Establish strong Executive S&OP (ES&OP) work process discipline: strict calendar, roles and responsibilities, deliverables, workflow, and so forth. This is needed due to the cross-functional nature of ES&OP and the need to make this a truly business-oriented process rather than a supply-chain process.

**RESULTS**

Between April, 2009 and December, 2010, Dow implemented their ES&OP Best Practices in over nine (9) of their businesses, as well other efforts associated with supply-chain planning. The BDS sub-team was able to deliver cost synergies associated with implementing S&OP Best Practices, as well as help enable revenue growth synergies.

Scott Winstead, who led the BDS sub-team in this effort and is currently a Supply Chain Improvement Director for a major Dow business, cited the experience of a specific business unit:

*One of the first businesses to adopt the Dow ES&OP Best Practice was Dow Microbial Control (DMC). As a growth business inside of the Dow Advanced Materials Division, the business leadership for DMC realized that an effective and efficient ES&OP process would be required to advance the global leadership position for the business.*

Bryan Kitchen, DMC Business Operations Director, said:

*ES&OP was used effectively to accelerate integration, improve our sustainability profile, manage complexities associated with running a global enterprise in dual ERP environments, optimize our total cost basis, and deliver world-class service improvements, all while delivering against unmatched growth in all world areas. We clearly believe in the power of "AND"[1]; the only way to get there is through effective and efficient business management processes like ES&OP that are built to translate strategy into operational plans.*

Here's Scott Winstead again:

*DMC continues to pioneer ES&OP process improvements within Dow by providing structural design requirements for our new ES&OP technology, as well as piloting the system. DMC expects additional service, cost, productivity, and working capital improvements through the full implementation of this integrated platform, and our new technology is prepared to deliver.*

On February 3, 2011, Dow cited the Rohm and Haas integration effort as having been completed a quarter earlier than originally planned and exceeding its original synergy targets:

" . . . Dow achieved its synergy commitments related to the acquisition of Rohm and Haas and reduced structural costs a full quarter ahead of schedule, with realized savings of $2.4 billion and an annual run-rate of $2.5 billion...."

Darrell Zavitz is Vice President, Supply Chain and Customer Services, Business Process Services and Six Sigma at Dow. Here's his view of what took place during and after the acquisition:

---

[1] An example of "the power of AND" is the ability to have high customer service AND low inventories instead of one OR the other.

*Implementation of Executive S&OP within our combined businesses played a significant role in helping to integrate the two companies. This was a driving force for realizing and enabling cost and growth synergies.*

*We are refining our ES&OP implementation methodology with innovative technology, so that it not only continues to evolve, but also to improve our overall demand management, our supply capability, and to balance demand and supply steps. This will provide additional value beyond the efforts that we've already completed in our ES&OP change management and work process activities.*

*   *   *   *   *

The moral of the story: It may be a bit of a coincidence that two of our first three cases are from the chemical industry, but perhaps not totally. You see, Dow is a highly accomplished user of Executive S&OP, as is BASF. And DuPont is also. Why? Are the problems more severe in the chemical business? Are their people smarter? Or harder working? Probably not. Capacity issues in chemical companies can be more complex than average, and that may have been an early incentive for them to adopt S&OP.

The Dow/Rohm and Haas experience may serve as a model for future mergers: Use Executive S&OP as the tool to achieve integration; it may be the fastest and surest way to get there.

Interestingly, one of the reviewers for this book, Procter & Gamble's Dick Clark said, "Dow's integration process and the good news/bad news examples are very reminiscent of P&G's experience with the Gillette acquisition." — TW

# Chapter 6

# Company: V&M Star

**Area of Focus:** **Long-Range Cash Flow Projections Based on Executive S&OP**

Author's comments: Two interesting things about this company: One, they make products for what's called the "oil patch" (that means the petroleum industry). This business, more than most, is subject to periodic booms and busts; it seems to be a way of life. While stationed with the U.S. Navy in South Texas over thirty years ago, I saw bumper stickers that said: "Lord, please give us one more boom — then we'll stop." As you might imagine, good forward visibility in a business like this can be a major plus.

The other aspect of this business that makes it a bit different is that they're part of a corporation based in Paris (France, not Texas).

---

## CASH FLOW PLANNING WITH EXECUTIVE S&OP

V&M Star
Houston, Texas
Products: Oil Field Equipment
Business Unit Sales Not Disclosed

This organization is a component of Vallourec & Mannesman Tubes, the world market leader in the manufacture of seamless hot-rolled steel tubes. In July 2002, the tubular division of North Star Steel was acquired by V&M and renamed V&M Star.

They implemented Executive S&OP in 2006/2007, at the urging of their Chief Financial Officer at the time, Adam Szczepanski, who had S&OP experience at a prior employer and was convinced that it would help solve many of the company's problems. The implementation was highly successful; although V&M Star is one of the smaller companies featured in this book, none of them have used it more effectively and intelligently to support their business.

Adam's belief is that forward-looking financial plans are far better when developed in conjunction with S&OP. He says:

*A finance model based on a revenue dollar forecast with a gross profit percentage is worthless. It's too general to drive specific strategies and tactics. It's usually a Finance exercise that has limited buy-in from operating folks and does not serve as a road map of the future.*

*On the other hand, S&OP provides the meaningful details and single set of numbers that ties strategies and tactics to the financial forecast. Further, the extended planning horizon of S&OP provides financial forecasting with an opportunity to address strategic alternatives.*

## THE BACKGROUND

The periodic booms and busts of the petroleum industry were one of the drivers at V&M to get into Executive S&OP in the first place. The company keenly felt the lack of good visibility beyond the next few months. They had a classic "bad news" situation:

1. The "up and down" nature of the oil patch business

2. Production processes that are very capital-intensive

3. The long lead times to acquire new equipment, sometimes one to two years, and

4. The lack of visibility that far into the future

One of the key aspects of this dilemma was cash. It was a typical demand/supply situation, one where Executive S&OP has been quite effective. Accurate and valid cash flow projections for 24 months, based largely on S&OP, became a key requirement, and it's made a big difference in how V&M Star people run the business.

DEMAND ⟵⟶ SUPPLY

How much cash would they need, for example, if they added substantial new equipment for the plant ?

How much cash could they expect in terms of future cash flow, this year and next ?

First, let's look at their financial integration process from a view of about 5,000 feet, as prepared by one of the key players, Melissa Takas. Melissa moved from Finance into Operations as Operations Controlling Supervisor, which she describes as a mix between industrial engineer and plant accountant.

In addition to the data shown in Figure 6-1, supporting schedules for raw and work-in-process inventory, cost of goods sold, utilities, SG&A, and so on are added to enable valid cash flow projections.

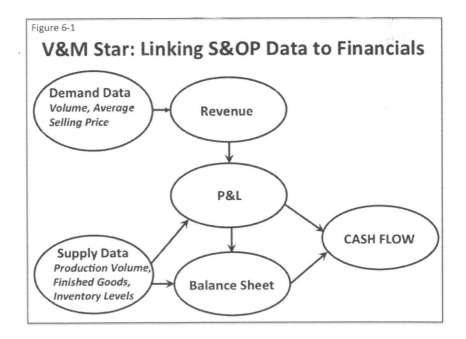

Figure 6-1

## V&M Star: Linking S&OP Data to Financials

## DODGING A BULLET

A few years back, the V&M Operations Department was planning a major shutdown to their Pipe Mill facility in Youngstown OH, expected to last 28 days and projected to improve processes and to increase capacity by 10%. In order to do this, they needed to pre-build this plant's output — to produce early and build inventory so that the company could continue to service its customers during the shutdown.

Well, inventory takes two things: space and money. Space was no problem because that inventory could be stored outside in the yard. Money proved to be another matter.

The production plan in Executive S&OP reflected the increased production, and the inventory plan showed a large increase in inventory. Everything looked okay until Melissa and her colleagues in Finance ran the S&OP cash flow projection and saw an enormous potential problem: They were going to run out of cash.

An important item entering the cash flow forecast from outside of Executive S&OP was a multi-million dollar dividend payment to the corporate office that V&M Star was required to make periodically. I'm sure that many of you readers will agree that in cases such as this, the corporate office usually takes priority. Furthermore, the V&M Star people felt that borrowing was not an option due to the cost.

The manager of the Melt Shop, a capacity-critical component of the Pipe Mill, was told that his production plan could not be funded. He rethought the planned pre-build of inventory, reworked the production plan, and he figured out how to do the upgrade in half the time. He had to get quite creative, but manufacturing people are good at that.

## HAPPY ENDING, HAPPY PEOPLE

Here's Melissa again on what happened:

*The April/May 2008 outage [plant shutdown] was completed on time and on budget. The outage impacted the Melt Shop for 14 days: 9 major capital projects were completed and various other lump sum and maintenance items were done as well. In early 2007, we started to see the impact that the outage would have on the inventory in April of 2008, and thus we were able to start planning a year in advance.*

*The outage was so successful that our customers didn't feel any effects from it. This was the pivotal event that showed us why we do S&OP — because it works!*

If V&M Star hadn't been doing the cash flow projection — *tied to Executive S&OP* — what would have happened? Chances are they would have discovered the cash crunch too late, meaning that perhaps the dividend payment to Paris would have been delayed, and/or the plans to upgrade the Pipe Mill would have slowed down dramatically, and/or the cost of borrowing would have wiped out much of the cost savings from the project.

Speaking to an S&OP conference in Chicago a few years ago, Melissa talked about their financial communications with Paris:

*We currently have two financial forecasts at our company. We have the S&OP plan, which is the internal forecast and the basis of how we run the business. We also have an external forecast that goes to Corporate for consolidation. The external forecast is generally a mirror image of S&OP with built-in safety factors for items such as average selling price and what we refer to as management judgment.*

*The S&OP forecast is revised monthly but the external forecast is revised only quarterly. When the external forecast is updated, it is based on the latest S&OP forecast with the safety factors I just mentioned.*

*In the past we would create a plan for the next fiscal year and we would be held to that plan. Now instead of having our shipments goal be based on the entire year (which would have been established in September of the prior year), we lock in quarterly shipping estimates and we are held to those numbers instead.*

One of the best endorsements of their Executive S&OP process came from the former V&M Star President and CEO, Roger Lindgren. I can remember sitting in a conference room at Ohio State with Roger, Adam, and the production planning manager Amy Mansfield before they began their implementation of Executive S&OP, discussing whether they should proceed. I could tell that Roger was skeptical and he'll readily agree with that.

Following implementation, Roger said:

*We now have our entire management team talking every month about what might happen 6 to 12 to 18 months out into the future and validating or modifying our plan. Wow! Why didn't we always do it this way?!*

\*   \*   \*   \*   \*

The moral of the story: This case bears out my belief that Executive S&OP's benefits to the Finance side of the business can be comparable to those on the Operational side. Adam Szczepanski is no exception: CFOs love this stuff once they've lived with it.

Let's revisit Adam's earlier quote: "A finance model based on a revenue dollar forecast with a gross profit percentage is worthless. It's too general to drive specific strategies and tactics . . . S&OP provides the meaningful details and single set of numbers that ties strategies and tactics to the financial forecast."

Yes indeed, Adam. — TW

# Chapter 7

# Company: Newell Rubbermaid

**Areas of Focus:**  **1. Business Unit/Corporate Collaboration**
**2. Advanced Demand Planning**

Author's comments: Many of us have heard the phrase, "I'm from the corporate office and I'm here to help you." We're aware that there's some cynicism here; on occasion corporate visitors have been less than highly helpful.

Happily, the reverse seems to be true with Executive S&OP. In this book, we see larger companies that have established central S&OP support staffs to assist the business units in implementing or improving their S&OP processes; Dow Chemical and Procter & Gamble have two of the longest running organizations of this type, and they have met with significant success over the years. But newer support units can add substantial value also. Read on.

---

## CENTRAL SUPPORT FOR IMPROVING FORECASTS

Newell Rubbermaid
Atlanta, Georgia
Products: Office and Home Products
Annual Sales: $5.8 bllion

A similar organization to the ones I just mentioned is the Supply Chain Excellence Group (SCEx) at Newell Rubbermaid, whose brands include Rubbermaid®, Sharpie®, Graco®, Irwin®, Paper Mate®, Goody®, Levolor®, and others.

SCEx has been deeply involved in the implementation of Executive S&OP within the Global Business Units (GBUs) and with post-implementation activities. For many companies, forecasting is the toughest part of operating S&OP successfully, so it's appropriate to explore SCEx's role in a forecasting improvement initiative.

I'm including this case for two reasons:

1. The importance of forecasting, as was just mentioned, and

2. To demonstrate the positive effect that a well-structured and well-staffed central group can have on business units operating Executive S&OP.

## BACKGROUND

In the latter stages of implementation at Newell Rubbermaid, the basic S&OP processes were taking hold across the company's GBUs and thus the SCEx group started to look ahead to what the next steps would be. They elected to develop a Community of Practice for developing and sharing best practices in the realm of forecasting.

The SCEx team felt an approach that simply dictated best practices would be unlikely to gain traction. That would seem too much like "I'm from the corporate office and I'm here to help you. This is what you need to do." The SCEx people knew the key would be to pull everyone together in a broad forecasting community to utilize their experience and generate excitement and buy-in for new ideas.

To jump start the process, SCEx formed a team of forecasting experts from across all GBUs, regions, and functions. The goal of the team was to:

• Develop a forecasting process that would deliver world-class forecasting accuracy.

• Develop advanced analytical techniques that would help each business optimize the forecasting process for the specifics of its supply chain.

- Develop a training program and assessment procedure to ensure continued forecasting excellence.

The scope of the effort was intentionally not limited to demand planning for replenishment items but included new products and promotional events; they are key drivers of business performance in some of the GBUs. The initiative was to focus on three general areas of improvement for forecasting and demand planning: People, Process, and Technology.

Since forecasting software was already installed, the SCEx people felt the focus should be more on the People and the Process elements with the intent of maximizing their ability with the current system instead of immediately looking for new, more "powerful" forecasting software. Efforts directed at developing new tools would be within the existing software environments.

The key supply chain metrics that the efforts addressed were:

- Inventory levels (safety stock and excess/obsolete)

- Customer service levels

- Forecast accuracy

    √  Overall accuracy (by SKU)

    √  Portfolio accuracy (measured as a percentage of SKUs with < +/– 20% error)

- Forecast bias

Let's hear from Sean Schubert, a member of SCEx and a key player in this initiative. Sean is the Senior Manager, Supply Chain, and has a strong background in continuous improvement and Six Sigma.

## FORECASTING DEEP DIVE TEAM

*Our first effort on the People side was to create a Forecasting Deep Dive team. Representatives were recruited from all GBUs and regions. Since forecasting is so integral to the business, it was essential to have representation from all key stakeholder groups; so we also recruited participants from other key functions in the business (Sales, Brand Marketing, Channel Marketing, Finance, etc.). This was especially key considering that some businesses are heavily driven by the performance of new products and promotions, whose forecasts are often generated in Marketing.*

*We brought the whole Forecasting Team together for a three-day Forecasting Summit. The goals were to: generate excitement, build a forecasting community, swap best practices, and introduce some new tools. The leaders of the team also spent time in advance researching cutting-edge tools and techniques for forecasting so these could be put in front of the community for consideration.*

*The specific topics covered during the first three-day meeting were:*

- *Forecast Accuracy Metrics*

- *Cost of Forecasting Error*

- *Forecast Value-Added Analysis*

- *Inherent Forecastability*

- *Wisdom of the Crowd Forecasting*

- *Collaborative Planning Forecasting and Replenishment (CPFR)*

*We spent two of the days Process Mapping the current and future state for three distinct forecasting situations:*

- *Replenishment*

- *New Products*

- *Promotional Events*

*These process maps were built more to drive discussion with the GBUs than to be used as a process compliance tool. For example, if a business feels they need to improve their New Product forecasting, then we would walk through the NPD forecasting process map with them to highlight gaps and opportunities in process, tools, and potential best practices from other businesses.*

*The Summit was a great success. There was great excitement in swapping best practices and the new tools discussed.*

## PITCH TO LEADERSHIP

At this point, SCEx wanted to ensure that leadership understood and supported these efforts, a critical factor because the improvement efforts would occur within the GBUs themselves. They explained the new tools and approach to GBU Supply Chain VPs, supply chain organizations being the ones most involved with the S&OP process.

In parallel, they briefed the Group Presidents, who oversee multiple GBUs, to ensure that if questions about the forecast accuracy initiative came up, they would be up-to-speed on the approach for improving forecasting and thus be in a position to drive change from above.

## RECAP

Several elements stand out in SCEx's approach:

- Forecasting Effectiveness Assessment, which enables tracking how well a given business unit's forecasting is performing. The questions are meant to be generic enough to find gaps in their process, but detailed enough to drive improvement and pull them towards some of the newer tools and analytics.

- Forecasting Effectiveness Workshops, centering on topics such as forecasting segmentation strategy, Forecast Value-Added

Analysis (see below), forecast accuracy and bias metrics, utilizing customer point-of-sale and inventory information, long-range forecasting out to 18 months and beyond, and others. This workshop was later broadened to include all of S&OP and renamed the "S&OP Effectiveness Workshop."

- Forecast Value-Added Analysis (FVA). This is a relatively new approach to forecasting;[1] it takes a novel approach to the forecasting problem in that it relates current forecasting results to the results from a "naïve" forecast, e.g., make next month's forecast the same as last month's actual sales.[2] In a very real sense, it applies the principles of Lean Manufacturing to forecasting and is being used by a growing number of companies, some of whom are featured in this book.

A number of the GBUs have made substantial progress in forecasting as a result of this initiative. One of them reported a 10% decrease in forecast error along with a 26% increase in finished inventory turns, a reduction in excess and obsolete inventory of 22%, and a 2.1% increase in perfect orders (a widely used measure of order fulfillment performance in the consumer goods industry).

Possibly best of all, Line Fill and On-Time percentages remained in the high 90% range as the inventory came down. Much of this performance flows directly from improved forecasts.

\*　　\*　　\*　　\*　　\*

The moral of the story: In large organizations, central S&OP support groups can make a big difference. We'll see more of them as an increasing number of large companies come to appreciate the power of Executive S&OP; as an investment, a central group such as this can generate a very big bang for the buck.

---

[1] See: *The Business Forecasting Deal* by Mike Gilliland. (2010). Hoboken, NJ: John Wiley & Sons.
[2] As a general rule, for Demand Planning people the key comparison for FVA is the statistical forecast to the naïve forecast, and for Sales & Marketing the key comparison is the final consensus demand forecast (from the S&OP Process) to the statistical forecast.

Also, if you face forecasting challenges (who doesn't?), you owe it to yourself to take a look at Forecast Value Added. It makes a lot of sense.
— TW

# Chapter 8

# Company: Applied Materials, Inc.

**Area of Focus:    New Product Launch**

Author's comments: One of the toughest things companies must deal with is the introduction of new products: Uncertainties abound, assumptions dominate the Demand Planning process, and usually there's a great deal at stake.

Can Executive S&OP help with New Product Introduction? Well, it should be able to; first, S&OP is largely a coordination tool and certainly new products cry out for effective coordination; second, S&OP helps people cope with change, which is a way of life as new products get launched. It's a natural fit.

Here's the story of a business based in Israel that is reaping great benefits from using Executive S&OP in its mission-critical process of introducing new products.

---

## EXECUTIVE S&OP SUPPORT FOR NEW PRODUCT LAUNCH

Applied Materials, Inc.
Santa Clara, California
Products: Equipment for the Manufacture of Semiconductors, Flat
          Panel Displays, Solar Photovoltaic Cells
Annual Sales: $9.5 billion (2010)

Applied Materials is a bit of an anomoly: a machinery manufacturer playing a large role in the world of high tech. They make the equipment by which Intel, Toshiba, IBM, Sunpower, Taiwan Semiconductor Manufacturing, and others make their products. Applied's products tend to be high value, low volume, and highly configurable.

As such, the company is towards the back end of the supply chain. I'm writing this book on a MacBook Pro, into which Apple installs Intel chips, which Intel made using equipment provided by Applied. Demand is cyclical and can be highly variable, with demand swings of up to 700% per quarter. This is one of the reasons why, in 2008, Applied started to implement Executive S&OP in its largest business, the Silicon Systems Group (SSG).

Of the company's 2010 revenue of $9.5 billion, it spent $1.1 billion on Research & Development. Unlike most companies in the high-tech world, Applied manufactures in-house, reflecting the fact that it makes high-tech machinery, not-high tech electronics. Its plants are in China, Germany, Israel, Italy, Singapore, Switzerland, Taiwan, and the United States.

## THE PDC STORY

This case will focus on Applied's business unit known as Process Diagnostics and Control (PDC). This unit develops, manufactures, markets, and supports process diagnostics and control equipment designed for semiconductor manufacturing processes. Located in Rehovot, Israel and employing over 900 people, PDC plays a significant role in enabling the production of the next generation of microchips.

PDC has been using S&OP for over 10 years, and its people feel quite good about what they've been able to accomplish.

One accomplishment is a sharp reduction in lead times to customers. Prior to being acquired by Applied Materials, the organization now called PDC had customer lead times in excess of one year; today they typically range from three to five months, on some occasions even less.

This is made possible by several factors that PDC pioneered within Applied: range forecasting, supplier collaboration, and what they call *Integrate-to-Order*, a variant on the finish-to-order processes used by, among others, Dell Computer (Build-to-Order), Procter & Gamble (Late-Stage Differentiation), and Dow Chemical (Blend-to-Order).

A disclaimer: The S&OP process at PDC is atypical. It does not follow the standard five-step process, no doubt reflecting in part the disproportionate share of capacity required by New Products.

## S&OP'S ROLE IN NEW PRODUCT LAUNCH AT PDC

One of the intriguing aspects here is that S&OP for New Products is managed using a separate but parallel process from Sustaining (existing) Products. Reasons for this include:

- New Products require increased attention due to the uncertainties and changes that are part and parcel of new product launch activity.

- New Products are so vitally important to PDC. In fiscal year 2010, about 40% of all PDC volume shipped was in products launched that year.

- The marketing function known as Global Product Management is very active in S&OP for New Products. New Products require a much stronger alignment with Product Management whereas Sustaining Products are managed through the standard sales channels.

- The General Manager is more directly engaged in the S&OP process for New Products, participating in some of the earlier steps which he does not do with Sustaining Products. This is done to ensure strategic/tactical alignment, which is not as large an issue as with Sustaining Products. New Products need to have a very strong alignment between customer penetration strategy and build/supply chain plans, as the financial risk is typically higher.

- New Products have specific planning and execution challenges that need to be addressed, one being adequate field support for first shipments.

- New Product S&OP covers the phasing out of products being replaced, to maintain positive P&L and balance sheet performance during the transition from the old to the new product.

- Integration of the range forecasting process with supply planning ensures that supply requirements are aligned with demand assumptions.

## KEY ROLES IN NEW PRODUCT S&OP

- PDC General Manager: Head of the entire PDC business

- S&OP Meeting Facilitator: Prepares, coordinates, and facilitates the meeting

- Global Product Management: Presents New Product Plans and alignment with penetration strategy

- Demand Planning: Ensures New Product Plans have been integrated into Demand Plans

- Finance: Captures financial results and implications

- Operations: Ensures readiness for New Product Build Plan

## INTEGRATION OF EXECUTIVE S&OP WITH PRODUCT LIFE CYCLE MANAGEMENT SYSTEM

Applied's PDC unit utilizes a form of the Stage-Gate process,[1] called *Phase-Gate* at PDC, for managing its product development activities.

---

[1] The Stage-Gate process is a technique for managing product development projects, among others. The activities to be performed are divided into stages separated by gates. For the project to move from one stage to another, it must meet the requirements to do so, and this is determined at the gate separating the current stage from the next.

Of particular interest to us here are Gates 3, 4, and 5, plus one more that we'll cover in a minute:

- Gate 3 verifies that the product has satisfied the Concept & Feasibility requirements and has received project approval.

- Gate 4 verifies that the product is ready to ship as an alpha and then a beta test version.

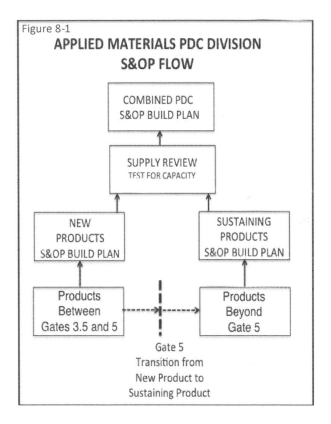

- Gate 5 verifies that the product is ready to transition from new product status to become a part of the sustaining, ongoing product line.

- Now for one more: Gate 3.5. This gate, positioned between Gates 3 and 4, says in effect that the product is sufficiently far along in its development that it can be brought into S&OP. See Figure 8-1.

  One of the main purposes of this gate is to establish that the product is mature at the component level (not the system as a whole) and Purchasing can thus proceed with minimum risk. This shortens the gap from Gate 4 to Gate 5 and gives an advantage in time-to-market.

  PDC has asked its key supplies to adopt the PDC phase-gate method. The suppliers are expected to always be one gate ahead of PDC. Thus, when PDC is in Phase 4, shipping beta product, the suppliers are already in Phase 5, producing at a volume production level. This gives the S&OP team the confidence to make procurement decisions, reduce risks, and shorten the overall process.

At this point, the New Product S&OP process has responsibility for this product until it moves through Gate 5, at which point the product is no longer considered a New Product but rather becomes a Sustaining one. The demand/supply planning role transfers to Sustaining S&OP.

The Supply Review meeting occurs following the New Product and Sustaining S&OP processes. Its purpose is to review and validate that capacity is available for the Build Plan. Adjustments are made as required, and the result is the basis for the combined, authorized Build Plan.

### RESULTS

Shelly Zafrir worked at PDC for nine years, during which time she led the implementation of S&OP there. In 2007, she was transferred to the Silicon Systems Group in Santa Clara, California as Sales & Operations Planning Director, but has remained in close contact with her former colleagues at PDC. Here's what Shelly told me about what they've accomplished:

*The folks at PDC are doing really well. They've come out of The Great Recession quite nicely, with dramatic increases in sales not only of sustaining products but also in the volume of new products that they've brought to market. Overall, unit shipments in 2011 are about four times what they were as recently as two years ago, in the middle of the downturn.*

*Simultaneously, manufacturing cycle time is dropping by about 15 to 20% on Sustaining Products. On New Products it's a great deal more, some of which is to be expected as the company comes down the learning curve. . . . but nowhere near all of the decrease is due to learning curve.*

*Also simultaneously, by Q2 of 2011 Excess and Obsolete Inventory had been reduced to less than half of its 2009 level and is expected to drop even further.*

*These positive developments are due largely to two things: an excellent S&OP process and a great team of people. I'd be remiss in not mentioning Miki Gruber, Yoav Shahak, Haim Kimel, Nachum Cohen, Nissim Haviv, and Udi Tzuri who helped greatly with the preparation of this case.*

★    ★    ★    ★    ★

The moral of the story: The successful introduction of New Products is so important to PDC that they treat them within S&OP separately but on a parallel path with Mature Products. To me, this is a strong validation of S&OP's effectiveness in supporting New Product Launch. — TW

# Chapter 9

# Company: Jarden Fresh Preserving

**Areas of Focus:**   1. **Risk Anticipation/Opportunity Enhancement**
2. **Advanced Demand and Supply Planning**

Author's comments: Many years ago, when I was young, preserving food at home was a big thing; my Mom did it every year and I "helped" her. We called it canning, although we used glass jars, not cans.

As you might imagine, the companies making the glass jars for canning have seasonal demand: high in the summer and low in the winter. Seasonal businesses can be difficult to manage and, of course, the more seasonal it is, the tougher it is. Some years ago, I worked with The Scotts Company, the folks who make lawn fertilizer and related products. Some of their product families sold over 90% of their annual volume in less than 90 days. It's intense.

We hear a lot about risk these days, much of it being supply chain risk, for example, when an earthquake and tsunami hit Japan in the Spring of 2011. Another type of risk, which we'll explore here, is market risk: What happens when the marketplace routinely wants substantially more than you're able to provide — or much less than you're geared up to provide?

---

## MANAGEMENT OF MARKET RISK THROUGH EXECUTIVE S&OP

Jarden Fresh Preserving
Daleville, Indiana
Products: Glass Jars and Lids
Business Unit Sales Not Disclosed

One of the big players in the preserving business has been the Ball® brand of home canning products, now distributed by Jarden Corporation, which has annual of $6 billion. Its products include Coleman®, Oster®, Sunbeam®, Mr. Coffee®, Rawlings®, Bicycle® Playing Cards, and many others.

Today Jarden's Fresh Preserving (FP) business unit sells glass canning jars and associated lids to customers such as Wal-Mart, Kmart, Target, Kroger, Food Lion, Lowe's, Ace Hardware, Tractor Supply, and so on. Demand is highly seasonal during mid-to-late summer, with a large percentage of annual volume shipping between May and August.

## WHY S&OP BECAME A PRIORITY

One of the key S&OP players at Jarden is Brad McCollum, Manager, Sales & Operations Planning. Brad gives the background:

*This business has been around for a long-time and as the company headed into the 2008 season, our models based on that lengthy history suggested we would see a relatively flat if not slightly declining season. As had been done for the many seasons prior, Supply Plans were almost entirely level-loaded around these volume level demand assumptions: building up inventories in the off-season to accommodate the high demand that outstrips capacity during the season, with overtime serving as the primary buffer beyond those assumptions.*

Towards the latter half of the 2008 season, they began to see consumption (sales through retailers) increase significantly. They began to utilize overtime to supply the increased demand, but as the growth increased even more above the prior year, they quickly saw shortages in their longer lead time raw materials, primarily glass and steel.

In hindsight, FP can see that demand was different from any prior year because, first, we were entering into The Great Recession; people were looking for lower cost sources of food, one of which was to grow or buy fresh food and then preserve it. Second were the consumer trends toward healthy eating, gardening, and natural foods. Since the company had never before experienced either of these, they were unforeseeable using the backward-looking historical demand models.

Here's Brad McCollum again:

*Ultimately, 2008 was a phenomenal growth year for the fresh preserving category and, unfortunately, a very painful year not only for the Jarden Fresh Preserving business but also for our customers and our end consumers.*

## FRESH PRESERVING S&OP DESIGN

After the experience in 2008, FP management elected to implement Executive S&OP and, further, to acquire an S&OP process with a demand model and supply model that allowed them to identify potential risks given different demand scenarios. With this, they reasoned, they could proactively plan mitigations where feasible, balancing customer service risks (fill rate, on-time delivery) with financial risks (working capital, EBIDTA[1]) and do so without passing those risks on to their labor force and/or vendors. More from Brad:

*Nothing in our historical data could have enabled us to predict the 2008 season, so it was critical that our S&OP demand model have forward-looking inputs based on extrinsic factors that we believed to be the drivers of the business. Key to this modeling process was to develop our ability to quantify those impacts, thereby:*

- *Reaching consensus each month about the forecast based on each of those factors and thus producing not only a consensus demand number but also . . .*

- *Developing a range of demand scenarios that were data driven, not opinion driven.*

---

[1]Earnings Before Interest, Depreciation, Taxes, Amortization

The result was a model that helped take the decades of experience the company has in this area and translate it into quantifiable impacts to demand. It allows them each cycle to discuss these factors that drive the business and debate the assumptions around those factors.

Their demand model and process ultimately requires debate and eventually alignment around not only factors such as distribution and promotion, but also the impacts of those key factors out of their control (i.e., weather, macroeconomic conditions, etc.). As a result, demand teams are able to offer supply teams not only a better forward-looking consensus demand plan, but also demand scenarios that represent where that forecast might likely be wrong and by how much.

## MODELING SUPPLY FLEXIBILITY

FP's supply model is designed around the constraints inherent within its supply capability, recognizing not only the normal variation that may occur within production, but also recognizing and modeling the flexibility that exists within the supply chain. Two important points:

1. Seasonal businesses usually have excess capacity in the off-season, so understanding the details of the excess is important when determining how much of that capacity to utilize. One way to mitigate volume risk is just to build a bunch of product early and trim back as the season comes in. Sometimes that is exactly the bet that one has to make.

   However, by understanding the flexibilities that do exist within the supply chain, one can better optimize that mitigation and possibly choose to make investments or make commitments to add flexibility where there would be benefit (i.e., labor flexibility, commitments with vendors to reserve material, capital equipment, and so forth).

2. Modeling constraints and flexibilities are necessary not only within the company itself, but also within that of its vendors.

Within FP, if they see scenarios that call for "x"% increase in demand for lids, they'll need more capacity to produce them but they'll also need more steel and other raw materials, and in some cases, potentially more storage or even distribution capacity.

If they don't exercise the scenario all the way through the supply chain, the FP people feel they really aren't mitigating anything; as the saying goes "the chain is only as strong as its weakest link." This deeper consideration within supply flexibility is based on the simple fact that capacity is useless without the raw materials and/or labor to utilize it.

## BRIDGING DEMAND TO SUPPLY

FP's Executive S&OP process operates with market-facing product families, the preferred method. Their supply models are grouped around supply chain constraints, so the process requires a translation from demand family to supply constraint. This translation is based on mix assumptions that need to be monitored each cycle as

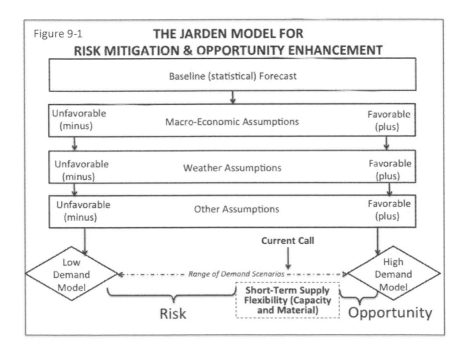

Figure 9-1 **THE JARDEN MODEL FOR RISK MITIGATION & OPPORTUNITY ENHANCEMENT**

well. Using run charts, the process monitors actual variation against the mix assumptions and the model is adjusted when appropriate. See Figure 9-1.

## SCENARIO PLANNING AND MITIGATION

With these models established and routinely verified and updated, FP is able to model various demand scenarios and apply them to a corresponding set of supply scenarios. Because they've stayed at a high level (market-facing families on the demand side and key constraint groupings on the supply side), this scenario planning takes minutes instead of days. They can quickly run a matrix of scenarios around the consensus demand and identify risk areas created by the potential error within the demand models.

Once this matrix has been populated, the Supply Management and Demand Management teams are able to discuss the probability of various risks, and then develop and propose plans to mitigate those risks. If they have downside demand risk, what can be done to ensure that extra promotional activities or other business stimulators are ready to be activated?

If high demand is projected and hence there will be insufficient supply, where can FP find additional capacities during key times, or do they have the working capital to utilize off-season capacities and build inventory to buffer that risk? How do they correct for those decisions if those buffers aren't needed and what impact will that have on key financials (working capital, EBITDA, etc.) as well as the labor force and vendor base? Let's hear from Brad McCollum one more time.

## RESULTS

*We began our implementation of Executive S&OP in January of 2009. That year we continued to see increased demand for our products and that year, as we all know, was again unlike any that we had seen before.*

*While S&OP didn't necessarily make us any better about predicting  the future, it did enable us to mitigate the risks that the inevitable error in our predictions would bring.*

*The year 2009 was again a great season for the fresh preserving marketplace, but this time we were able to service our growing business with significant improvements. Measures of on-time and complete shipments increased between 6 and 10%. And our improvements were not lopsided, because we also saw an 11% increase in inventory turn rates. Better service with less inventory — ultimately we delivered on-time and complete 98% of the time in a year that was very different from the years prior and we continue to do so across the business.*

Bob Stahl has first-hand experience with this company, so let's  hear a few words from him:

*As I wrote in the foreword to this book, the state of the art in this field is advanced by the practitioners, a living example of which is Jarden Fresh Preserving. I started working with them as the teacher, but quickly they built on best practice and got far beyond the basics. Today, as a result of their work with Executive S&OP, they are doing better than ever in spite of these difficult, uncertain times.*

★ ★ ★ ★ ★

The moral of the story: Simulation refers to the process of testing multiple scenarios to obtain a superior solution. The basics of S&OP would say to do this when there is a capacity constraint: You can't make enough to meet the demand — or when you don't have enough demand to meet the supply and thus need to know which production plan would be  the least disruptive, cause the fewest layoffs, etc.

This is the second example we've seen of a company doing simulation as a normal part of their S&OP process, the first being BASF. It's an inherent, routine part of their process, rather than the more typical S&OP approach of something that's done to address a specific problem. Simulations become a way of life. — TW

# Chapter 10

# Company: Staples

## Area of Focus:    Executive S&OP in Retail

Author's comment: The applications of S&OP have gradually been spreading. We see it being used in retail, distribution, banks, engineering groups, and other organizations that don't produce a physical product. A key consideration is: Do they have a challenge in predicting demand and balancing supply with it? If yes, S&OP is probably a fit.

---

## S&OP IN ON-LINE RETAIL

Staples, Inc.
Framingham, Massachusetts
Products: Office Equipment and Supplies
Annual Sales: $24.5 billion (2010)

Staples is the world's largest office products company, with sales generated by three primary business units: Delivery ($9.8 billion), Retail ($9.5 billion), and International ($5.2 billion).

Here we'll focus on the North American Delivery business, which has grown four-fold in the last ten years to the point where Staples claims second-place worldwide in e-commerce sales. It consists of three sub-units:

- Staples Business Delivery — sells to small businesses and home offices, primarily through Staples.com

- Staples Advantage — business-to-business division serving larger businesses, including Fortune 1,000 companies

- Quill — a wholly-owned office products subsidiary of Staples North American Delivery

Each business unit has its own structure and teams: Sales, Marketing, Pricing, Finance, and Merchandising.[1] However, these teams share the same supply chain: Inventory Management, Fulfillment, and Delivery. The process that we call Executive S&OP was established to synchronize the demand from these three business units with the one supply entity.

## THE PROCESS

The S&OP process consists of a monthly cycle grounded upon three distinct activities:

- Demand — A formal process to aggregate demand from each of the three business units into "one number of the truth"

- Supply — A formal process to translate this "one number of the truth" into supply plans such as vendor purchases, capacity, labor, and transportation plans

- Capabilities — Provide a forum for cross-functional and cross-business unit initiatives to be discussed and tracked. A graphic display of the complete process is shown in Figure 10-1.

There are two differences between this diagram and what you may be accustomed to. One concerns merely format: This is a circular S&OP diagram, rather than the linear, stair-step approach used by many. It makes no difference; both say the same thing.

The second difference: Figure 10-1 shows an S&OP process not for a manufacturer, but for a retail organization's Delivery Business Unit.

Well, there really aren't any major differences: First, they get the demand in focus (Steps 1 through 3), then bring in the supply picture and balance with demand (4 through 6), and then do what we call the Pre-Meeting and Exec Meeting (Step 7).

---

[1] In a retail environment, Merchandising is generally responsible for product assortment, promotions, and pricing. Marketing often works closely with Merchandising to help develop promotional activities and generate the resources (flyers, catalogs, coupons, e-mails, etc.) to support them.

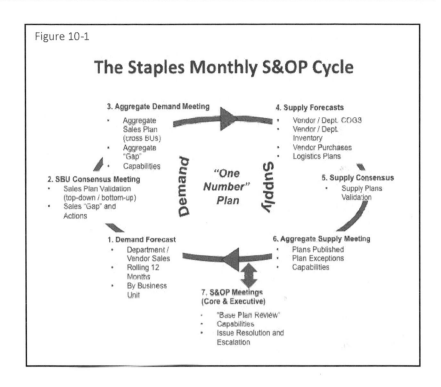

Figure 10-1

## The Staples Monthly S&OP Cycle

**3. Aggregate Demand Meeting**
- Aggregate Sales Plan (cross BUs)
- Aggregate "Gap"
- Capabilities

**4. Supply Forecasts**
- Vendor / Dept. COGS
- Vendor / Dept. Inventory
- Vendor Purchases
- Logistics Plans

**2. SBU Consensus Meeting**
- Sales Plan Validation (top-down / bottom-up)
- Sales "Gap" and Actions

*"One Number" Plan*

Demand    Supply

**5. Supply Consensus**
- Supply Plans Validation

**1. Demand Forecast**
- Department / Vendor Sales
- Rolling 12 Months
- By Business Unit

**6. Aggregate Supply Meeting**
- Plans Published
- Plan Exceptions
- Capabilities

**7. S&OP Meetings (Core & Executive)**
- "Base Plan Review"
- Capabilities
- Issue Resolution and Escalation

Folks, there are far more similarities here than differences. Perhaps the largest difference is that the basic unit of measure here is dollars, not units, which are used in most manufacturing companies.[2] At Staples, units play a part only on key critical SKUs, which are "micro-forecasted" in units, translated into dollars, and then rolled into the macro department forecast.

## AGGREGATE DEMAND PROCESS

Let's take a closer look at several of the key steps along the way. The process for Aggregate Demand culminates in a monthly meeting (Step 3) where the following are reviewed and discussed for each business unit:

- Most recent period's performance to forecast (both 1- and 3-month lags)

---

[2] In retail businesses, dollars are widely used as they're often the only common unit of measure within a given product grouping.

- Upcoming 12-month forecasts, including the consolidated numbers for all three businesses. This is relatively new for Staples, as it is for many new users of Executive S&OP; it's done to give improved visibility into future capacity needs, in this case, primarily warehouse space.

- "Gaps" to submitted forecasts and plans to mitigate those gaps, the gap being the difference between the forecast generated by the Demand Planning and Merchant teams versus the consensus forecast submitted to corporate. These gaps are monitored and reported on by the S&OP team over time.

- Upcoming promotional and seasonal events by business unit, specifically driven by Marketing, Merchandising, and Sales. This is done primarily for cross-business awareness.

## AGGREGATE SUPPLY PROCESS

This process also culminates in a monthly meeting (Step 6) where the following are reviewed and discussed:

- Supply plans based on the most recent demand plans, including Vendor Purchase Plans and Logistics Plans (warehouse space, transportation, labor, etc.).

- Supply Constraints, whether inventory or building capacity. The sales forecast is translated from dollars into carton/case counts, cubic feet, and labor hours.

- "Capability" Updates. These are cross-functional and/or cross-business unit initiatives that are facilitated, not executed, by S&OP. They include:

    √ Process improvement initiatives

    √ Annual events (catalog introduction, seasonal events such as back-to-school, Holiday, and so forth)

√ Cost vs. benefit analysis, for example, is it cheaper to stock a product in the field or to source it directly from the wholesaler?

√ New business initiatives and how they will differ from the existing product mix. For example, an upcoming major move into the Facilities and Break Room category will require a higher proportion of bulky paper products such as toilet tissues and towels. Reflecting this mix shift in cubic feet at the warehouses is important, as it does not always correlate to sales dollar shifts.

√ External Relationships (supplier or customer shifts)

At the conclusion of each monthly cycle, the monthly output from Steps 1 through 6 and prior goes to the two meetings in Step 7.

First is the **Core Team meeting**. This is like the functional equivalent of what's often called the Pre-Meeting. It includes, among others, VP-level demand and supply functional leads, who review the latest demand/supply plans and capabilities, plus resolve constraints that have been escalated up to them.

Next is the **Executive Team meeting**. The players here include the President of North American Delivery, Senior VP heads of the three business units, and the Senior VPs of Finance and Supply Chain. This session is to provide full transparency to gaps and issues; it includes a review of latest cycle plans, resolution of constraints escalated up to them, and resolution of roadblocks for process improvement.

## BENEFITS

Kristoffer Lutz, who's the Director of Sales & Operations Planning for Staples, says this about benefits:

*Hard benefits include the traditional ones when you forecast more accurately: higher in-stock positions with lower inventories, increased revenue due to lost sales avoidance, decreased service expense, and better working capital and cash flow.*

*Soft benefits are communication and teamwork. Teams discuss items together much earlier and in more detail than they ever did before. This makes for a more nimble organization and one where ideas and initiatives can be executed faster and with greater precision.*

## CONCLUSION

In terms of process, my conclusions are, first, that Staples has a very solid, first-rate S&OP process in place in their North American Delivery business.

Secondly, as I said earlier, there are far more similarities than differences when this process is compared to S&OP in a manufacturing business. Further, this applies not only to process similarities but also to implementation issues.

Talking about the major challenges in their implementation, Kris Lutz cited things such as change management, the absolute need for education to address the WIIFM[3] factor and the inevitable "yeah buts" that arise and, last but not least, persistence and continuous improvement:

*You have to keep at it cycle after cycle and constantly ask yourself if you are improving month over month. The process change you are rolling out is huge and people tend to jump on the bandwagon at various times. Once they see the value that demand and supply synchronization brings, they won't ever look back!*

*   *   *   *   *

The moral of the story: When I read this quote from Kris, I thought, "Gee, I could be talking to someone in a manufacturing company." That's a great quote. Kris is saying that the magnitude of the change is very large;

---

[3] "What's In It For Me?"

not everyone "comes to the party" at the same time; but when they get on board, they'll be on board forever. Most often, that's how it happens.

The bottom line is that this S&OP stuff works in retail and in distribution, in addition to companies that make things. The similarities are far greater than the differences. — TW

# Chapter 11

# Company: Procter & Gamble

**Areas of Focus:** **1. Measuring S&OP Effectiveness**
**2. Support for Earnings Calls**
**3. Global S&OP**

Author's comments: P&G has a habit of doing things well, a good thing for Executive S&OP in a company with one of the most complex global S&OP processes anywhere. Given that, and the company's desire to base its earning calls on S&OP-generated data, it was deemed essential that all of the company's many business units be exactly on the same page. Let's see how they accomplish that.

---

## S&OP SCOREKEEPING AT PROCTER & GAMBLE

The Procter & Gamble Company
Cincinnati, Ohio
Products: Consumer Packaged Goods
Annual Sales: $82.6 billion (2010)

Procter & Gamble is a large, complex company with 300 unique brands supported by operations in 80 countries, plants in 40 countries, and sold worldwide.

Let's start with a quote from Dick Clark, Associate Director in P&G's Global Supply Network Operations group and a key player in the evolution of S&OP at the company since the mid-1990s:

*S&OP plays a substantial role; it is one of the — some might say the — primary planning processes used to run the business.*

Executive S&OP operates along two axes, one product-focused — the three global business units: Beauty and Grooming, Health and   Well-

Being, and Household Care. The other axis is based on geography: the five regions around the world.

The plans for the businesses and the regions cover an 18-month horizon and are aligned into a single volume plan by business unit and market. These projections are used by Supply and Finance and are communicated to executive management, including the CEO; they form the basis for the quarterly earnings calls to Wall Street.

## THE GLOBAL S&OP PROCESS

P&G has worked hard to establish — and maintain — one standard monthly Executive S&OP process for *all businesses* around the world. And, since the process is standard for all users, the metrics are standardized as well.

Many business functions play important roles in the process, but Demand Planning, Supply Planning, and Financial Planning people are critical in leading the details of the process. These planners are co-located with the business units; together they evaluate scenarios and deliver plans to enable business success.

Specific roles and responsibilities include:

- The General Manager leads the overall process to deliver business results, making decisions and providing direction that supports the standard processes and a culture of transparent, unbiased planning.

- The Sales Leader ensures that Go-to-Market strategies are leveraged and in-sync with Business Operating Strategy and verifies that Sales inputs are timely, complete, and unbiased.

- The Finance Leader sees that the Profit Forecasting Process is fully integrated and in sync with the S&OP process, and ensures that Finance inputs are timely, complete, and unbiased.

- The Marketing Leader embraces S&OP as a key decision-making process; leads the process to identify business building opportunities; and ensures that Marketing inputs are timely, complete, and unbiased.

- The Business Analyst provides perspective on consumer habits and market trends, and ensures that Business Intelligence tools are fit for use and integrated into the S&OP process.

- The Demand Planning Leader verifies that key assumptions are aligned and included in the volume forecast, and ensures that the volume forecast is validated to be complete, realistic, and unbiased.

- The Supply Planning Leader ensures that the Supply Network assessment and Scenario Planning processes are in place to support S&OP, providing input and perspective on supply opportunities and constraints.

The S&OP process focuses on region/business unit combinations with a "matrixed" aggregation, as shown in Figure 11-1. Please note

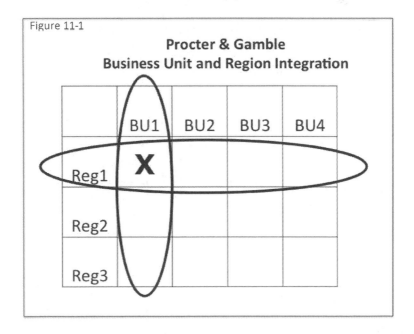

Figure 11-1

**Procter & Gamble**
**Business Unit and Region Integration**

the cell with the X, indicating the intersection between the total Sales & Operations Plan for Business Unit 1 and the total Plan for Region 1.

This implies that the Business view and the Region view are in harmony:

Region 1's forecast of what it expects to sell of
Business Unit 1's products

is equal to

what Business Unit 1 expects Region 1
to sell of its products

This process is followed across all businesses and regions, ensuring that both views — business and region — are in sync for the entire corporation, thus yielding one set of numbers with which to run the business internally.

## THE S&OP ASSESSMENT PROCESS

It's easy now to see why P&G expends substantial effort in assessing how and how well the Executive S&OP process is being done: Without this effort, it's almost certain that the individual businesses and regions would drift apart in their use of the process and thus the single-number process would not be possible.

Furthermore, such a "drifting apart" would degrade the validity of the financial numbers generated by the S&OP process, possibly to the extent that they would not be usable in the generation of financial projections and related earnings calls.

Also very important, the S&OP Assessment points the way to better results, serving as a primary element in continuous improvement. It does this by communicating expectations — "Here's how your S&OP process should perform" — and by providing a structure to evaluate current capacity and to define the gaps — "Here's how well you're currently doing and here's what needs to improve." It gives   a framework for development of the improvement plan: "Here's what needs to be done to get to where you need to be."

## HOW IT'S DONE

At P&G, the Global S&OP process is governed by a small group of Global Process Leaders (e.g. Demand Planning, Supply Planning). Their role, among other things, is to serve as the "owners" of the assessment process and its checklist.

Here are the major components of the process:

- **Global process capability teams**. Each global process has a network of business leaders and process experts that provide training and coaching, and also help ensure calibration and alignment on the process. Through this calibration and alignment, they become qualified to assess other businesses. These networks have a dotted-line link to the Global Process Leader.

- **Process excellence defined through a series of statements**. These statements not only define process excellence, but describe key principles and expectations of the work process. They are structured to describe the process that should be followed. For example, a statement might be, "All forecasts of future volume start with a statistical forecast" or "There is a clear monthly calendar with key meeting dates defined at least six months in advance."

- **Annual self-assessment by the business units**. Each business unit — a region or a market — does a self-evaluation using the assessment tool. This provides an opportunity to review expectations and current performance and to prepare for a validated assessment.

- **Annual validated assessment with qualified assessors**. Following a self-assessment, a business unit is assessed by one or more qualified assessors, people from a different business or perhaps a different region. Working across business units helps maintain understanding and alignment, and provides opportunities to reapply best practices.

- **Assessment interviews and document reviews.** To understand and align on capability, the assessor will conduct interviews with business leaders, review documentation related to the expectations of the assessment tool, and may attend the S&OP meeting for the business.

- **Assessment summary.** This step is to identify key strengths, opportunities, and the action plan, and it includes a score to aid in tracking performance over time. But, of more importance, it identifies key strengths that can be leveraged and opportunity areas for better performance. The assessor will coach the business on developing an action plan for improvement.

The S&OP Assessment is based on the Oliver Wight ABCD Checklist with substantial modifications to fit the company. It consists of six process sections:

1. **Leadership:** business unit leaderships' commitment to S&OP excellence and demonstrated support for education and training.

2. **Operating Strategy:** the content of the written business unit operating strategy, multi-functional engagement in the creation of the operating strategy, and clear examples that the operating strategy is a "living document" used to guide the business.

3. **Initiative Planning:** innovation strategy development, portfolio master planning, resource planning and decision making for new products, and innovation management and delivery.

4. **Demand Planning:** developing and communicating the volume forecast. Accountability for the forecasting process and key inputs to the forecast.

5. **Supply Planning:** rough-cut capacity planning and scenario planning.

6. **S&OP:** overall Supply Chain results, integration with Finance, and execution of the S&OP meetings and process.

Each section has about twenty statements that describe excellence in that area. These areas are probed by three types of statements or questions dealing with (a) work process, (b) capability, or (c) measures of results. Examples follow.

An example of a work process statement is, "The General Manager and leadership from each functional area seldom miss a meeting, substitutes are empowered to act and contribute to the process, and all involved parties view the meetings as critical to the business."

An example of a capability question is, "The General Manager and the business unit leadership team fully understand the concept of, the principles of, the benefits of, and the requirements of a Sales & Operations Planning Process."

An example of a measures question is, "Sales Plan Performance (by family and in total) is tracked and has been within tolerance (as defined in the Category Operating Strategy) at least 8 of the last 12 months."

Dick Clark points out that while the numeric scores resulting from the assessment are important:

*. . . the assessment process is really not about scores; it's about improvement plans. However, numbers are necessary: A number on a scorecard creates focus and enables not only the identification of gaps but also of outstanding performance. It also enables tracking performance over time. Together, this leads to process improvement and improved business results.*

*S&OP is a critical planning process at two levels. Operationally, it gives visibility to plans and ensures that we can balance a variety of demand*

*and supply considerations. From a business planning standpoint, the S&OP process enables collaboration and transparency with a variety of commercial business partners, ensuring proper links to financial planning and key business decision making.*

★    ★    ★    ★    ★

The moral of the story: P&G has perhaps the best S&OP process in the world. If not, it has to be in the top three. One of the impressive things about it is that S&OP extends all the way up to the ultimate corner office, that of the corporate Chief Executive Officer. Let me repeat Dick's quote from earlier: "S&OP plays a substantial role; it is one of the — some might say *the* — primary planning processes used to run the business."

Another impressive aspect is metrics. I can assure you that P&G would be nowhere near as good as they are if it weren't for the assessment process so superbly managed by Dick Clark and his colleagues. To those of you who don't have an effective S&OP assessment process, I urge you to get one. It can make a big, perhaps huge, difference in how well your business operates. — TW

# Chapter 12

# Where Are We and What's Coming?

We need to look at this topic along four dimensions:

1. Where is Executive S&OP now?

2. Where is your company now, relative to S&OP?

3. What's in the future for Executive S&OP?

4. What's in the future for your company, relative to S&OP?

We'll focus on them one at a time.

## Where Is Executive S&OP Now?

In other words, what's the state-of-the-art? Well, you know the state-of-the-art in S&OP; it's what you've been reading about in this book:

√ It's V&M Star generating S&OP-based cash flow projections for over a year into the future, thereby seeing a major cash shortage out there and taking corrective action well ahead of the potential problem becoming real; thereby keeping the corporate office in Paris happy by making the dividend payment on time.

√ It's Cisco Systems using S&OP intensively to help them develop an entirely new business and product line, one very different from what they're accustomed to, with superb results in the areas of customer service and inventory levels.

√ It's BASF, becoming number one in the chemical business and identifying S&OP as having "contributed significantly to helping us achieve our present position in the industry."

√ It's Procter & Gamble, with an extremely complex global business, using S&OP metrics to help coordinate an extremely large number of businesses, resulting in the development of key    data for quarterly earnings calls to Wall St. based on consolidated S&OP projections.

√ It's Dow Chemical, using Executive S&OP to help facilitate and integrate a $9 billion set of businesses with their existing ones, and thereby achieving cost and growth synergy targets set by corporate — and in some cases, surpassing them.

and ditto for Applied Materials, Jarden, Newell Rubbermaid, and Staples.

## Where Is Your Company Now, Relative to S&OP?

There are six possibilities:

1. **You're not using it and have no plans to do so.** This is not a good place to be unless you're sure that you're competitors are not using it now nor will they use S&OP in the future. There's a strong parallel between S&OP and Lean Manufacturing; if Lean is being used effectively by your main competitor(s) and you don't have it, you are at a substantial competitive disadvantage or will be soon. Ditto for Executive S&OP.

2. **You're implementing it.** Good. The principle of "do it right the first time"[1] applies here. The best number of times to implement S&OP is one (per business unit).

3. **You're operating it and you're not happy with it.** And that's almost certainly because you didn't implement it properly. Go to the next step.

4. **You're re-implementing it, because you're not happy with it.** The steps in a re-implementation are largely the same as with a first-time implementation. And please, do it right this time.[2]

---

1 For Bob Stahl's and my view of a virtually bulletproof implementation process, see *Sales & Operations Planning: The How-To Handbook, Third Edition, Wallace and Stahl, 2008.*
2 Ditto.

5. **You're operating it and you're happy with it.** Good, but don't stop there. Go to Step 6.

6. **You're operating it, you're happy with it, and you are implementing a major enhancement, designed to help run the business better.** This should be happening virtually all the time, and it's not just continuous improvement; it's continuous enhancement, not just doing the same stuff better but doing brand new things. This should become a way of life, one reason being that as the business changes, S&OP must change also in order to support the people running the business. That's it's job.

## What's in the Future for Executive S&OP?

From the view of this admittedly biased observer, the future looks quite bright. Executive S&OP will continue to grow, not only in power and scope but also in the number of user companies. Some reasons:

- **The Adoption Curve**, discussed in Chapter 1 and in Appendix A.

- **Success breeds success** or, said another way, the word gets around. One example: the vice president/general manager of Division A gets promoted to the role of executive vice president of Group 3, which contains five divisions. This person is an S&OP believer; she's seen it work wonderfully in Division A. Therefore, in her new role, she "encourages" the heads of the five divisions to explore and consider Executive S&OP.

- **Lean Manufacturing and S&OP**. The Lean community has discovered S&OP and many are flocking to it. The reason: variable demand. Many Lean users got their training and consulting from persons who worked at Toyota Manufacturing, Well, Toyota does not have much of a problem with variable demand because they ship directly to a group of happy, contented, wealthy Toyota dealers who are not inclined to make waves with the factory.

However, most companies ship to customers whose demand varies and are usually not happy or contented, but rather, can be quite demanding. People who supply these customers are finding that they need S&OP, no matter how good they are with Lean.

- **Globalization**. As businesses become more and more global, they're harder to coordinate. S&OP is essentially a coordination tool, perhaps the best one around, and is meeting with substantial success when deployed globally.

- **New users outside traditional manufacturing** are being to added to the ranks of S&OP users. Staples, Radio Shack, Office Max, and the National Australia Bank have been early adopters.

- **S&OP specific software**. We haven't talked about S&OP-specific software yet, so this is an opportunity to do so. First, contrary to what some people would have you believe, it's possible to do Executive S&OP with spreadsheet software, e.g., Excel®. Some of the companies in this book do it this way. The good news is that there's no additional cost and your people already know it.

  However, spreadsheet software can take you only so far; sooner or later you'll probably find that you need S&OP-specific software to do everything you want to do. There is some first-rate S&OP-specific software out there and that's giving impetus to the growth of Executive S&OP, both in numbers of users and capabilities.

- **A growing presence in the executive suite**. We've seen examples of that in this book, and we'll see more examples in the future. Basing earnings calls on S&OP projections and using S&OP 18-month plans as the basis for next year's annual plan are but two examples.

## What's in the Future for Your Company, Relative to S&OP?

I can't answer that; it's up to you. But I do have a thought I'd like to leave with you.

This book's title includes the words *Beyond the Basics.* While every company in this book is doing advanced S&OP-based processes, we must not lose sight of the fact that they are doing the basics very well. They continuously keep demand and supply in balance, and they can see both units and dollars in their S&OP information.

Why is that important? Because if the numbers in Executive S&OP don't show demand and supply in balance, the rest of the numbers don't mean anything. They'll be wrong, because the numbers they're based on are suspect.

★    ★    ★    ★    ★

The moral of the story: Get the basics right before you try to go beyond them. Walk before you run. Then, run!

Thanks for listening.

Tom Wallace
Cincinnati, Ohio
www.TFWallace.com

# APPENDIX A

# The Great Terminology Brouhaha

The terminology in this field is not good. We have a hodge-podge of competing terms and acronyms:

- *Sales & Operations Planning*

- *Executive S&OP*

- *S&OP*

- *Integrated Business Planning*

- *SIOP* (Sales, Inventory, and Operations Planning)

and a new one I heard recently

- *SOIP* (Sales, Operations, and Inventory Planning, I suppose).

Surprise! With one exception, they all mean pretty much the same thing; the differences are far fewer than the similarities.

So what's the one exception? Another surprise perhaps, it's the term *Sales & Operations Planning,* which formerly referred to an executive-centered decision-making process focusing on *volume* issues (see diagram). This process utilizes techniques for Demand Planning/ Forecasting and Supply/Capacity Planning to accomplish its mission.

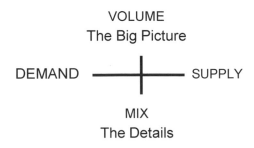

However, the meaning of the term *Sales & Operations Planning* has morphed; it's broadened into something larger than it was originally. That may sound positive, but trust me, it's not. Today, many people view S&OP as dealing with *mix* in addition to volume. Thus it now can include Master Scheduling and other mix-related tools such as customer order promising, distribution replenishment, supplier scheduling, plant scheduling, and more — sometimes done via the use of Advanced Planning Systems, sometimes with Kanban.

Some are predicting that Sales & Operations Planning, in the larger sense, will become the successor term to Enterprise Resource Planning, which today is seen by most to mean software, as in *ERP software*. Okay fine, but in the meantime, we have a problem.

This morphing of the term *Sales & Operations Planning* has generated confusion: People today frequently don't know if a person is talking about the volume component of Sales & Operations Planning (the old meaning) or is including the detailed mix pieces (the morphed term). Sometimes we wonder if the person using the term even knows what he or she means!

## EXECUTIVE S&OP

So, since Sales & Operations Planning now means more than the executive process, how is the executive process to be identified?

Well, consistent with the principle of keeping it simple, we call it *Executive S&OP*. Therefore, Sales & Operations Planning — the larger entity — has the following component parts: Executive S&OP, Demand Planning, Supply (capacity) Planning, along with Master Scheduling and related detail-level tools for the managing of mix.

Executive S&OP is a volume-focused decision-making tool for top management.

## S&OP

I use the term *S&OP* as having the same meaning as *Executive    S&OP*. It's merely a form of verbal shorthand.

## INTEGRATED BUSINESS PLANNING

I'm not totally sure what this means, but the best I can figure out is that *Integrated Business Planning* is mostly *Executive S&OP* with perhaps some additional emphasis on new product development issues. Here again, the similarities are much, much more numerous and concrete than the differences.

## SIOP

This one goes mainly by its acronym, which means *Sales,    Inventory, & Operations Planning.* The term *SIOP* was first used, to the best of my knowledge, at Allied Signal and then its use broadened with the Allied/Honeywell merger and also as Allied people moved to other companies and took the term with them.

I have never seen a rigorous definition of *SIOP* or the term to follow, but my understanding is that they're just about identical to *Executive S&OP.*

## SOIP

I suppose this means *Sales, Operations, & Inventory Planning.* Whatever.

# APPENDIX B

# Coming Up the Adoption Curve

S&OP was invented around 1980, and required 20 or more years to become popular. Why? What took so long?

Actually, that time span — 15 to 25 years — is fairly normal. There seems to be a 20-year time lag, plus or minus, between the development of a new process and its widespread implementation. Some examples:

- Manufacturing Resource Planning and its successor Enterprise Resource Planning came together in the early 1970s but hit a high adoption rate only in the 1990s.

- Total Quality Management/Six Sigma emerged at around the same time but here also, it took several decades for it to reach critical mass.

- Just-in-Time/Lean Manufacturing came over from Japan in the 1980s but really didn't get widely popular until around 1995 or so.

This can be depicted graphically by what's called the "Adoption Curve."

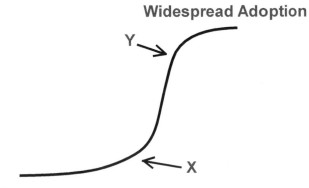

**Widespread Adoption**

Y

X

**Initial Development**

The period from Initial Development to Point X is one of slow but usually steady growth, as the word gets around and more companies start to use the process. Point X is the upward inflection point: The adoption rate steepens sharply and before long, most companies are trying to do it, some successfully and some not so much, in the rush to get on the bandwagon.

Point Y is the point of leveling; the adoption rate slows and growth is mainly a function of increase in the number of companies that are candidates for the process.

As this is written, Executive S&OP is between Points X and Y, probably a bit closer to Y.

# Resource Material

## Books

Wallace, Thomas F. and Robert A. Stahl, *Sales & Operations Planning – The How-To Handbook*, *3rd Edition*. Cincinnati, OH: T.F. Wallace & Company, 2008.

Wallace, Thomas F. and Robert A. Stahl, *Sales Forecasting: A New Approach*. Cincinnati, OH: T.F. Wallace & Company, 2002.

Wallace, Thomas F. and Robert A. Stahl, *Master Scheduling in the 21st Century*. Cincinnati, OH: T.F. Wallace & Company, 2003.

Wallace, Thomas F. and Robert A. Stahl, *Sales & Operations Planning: The Self-Audit Workbook*. Cincinnati, OH: T.F. Wallace & Company, 2008.

Wallace, Thomas F. and Robert A. Stahl, *Building to Customer Demand*. Cincinnati, OH: T.F. Wallace & Company, 2005.

Dougherty, John and Christopher Gray, *Sales & Operations Planning – Best Practices*. Vancouver, BC: Trafford Publishing, 2006.

Palmatier, George E. and Colleen Crum, *Enterprise Sales & Operations Planning*. Boca Raton, FL: J. Ross Publishing, 2003.

Crum, Colleen and George E. Palmatier, *Demand Management Best Practices: Process, Principles, and Collaboration*. Boca Raton, FL: J. Ross Publishing 2003

# GLOSSARY

**Aggregate Forecast** — See: **Volume Forecast.**

**Aligned Resources** — Resources that match up very closely with the product families. For example, all of the production for Family A is done in Department 1 and Department 1 makes no product for any other family; similarly for Family B and Department 2, and so on. Determining future capacity requirements for aligned resources is simpler than for matrix resources. See: **Unaligned Resources.**

**Assemble-to-Order** — See: **Finish-to-Order.**

**Bias** — The amount of forecast error build-up over time, plus or minus. This is a measure of over forecasting or under forecasting. See: **Running Sum of Forecast Errors.**

**Bill of Resources** — A listing of the important resources required to produce and deliver a given product or product family. Used in **Resource Requirements Planning** and **Rough-Cut Capacity Planning**.

**Build-to-Order** — Term popularized by Dell Computer; it has a similar meaning to **Finish-to-Order** and **Assemble-to-Order.** See: **Finish-to-Order.**

**Business Plan** — The financial plan for the business, extending out three to five fiscal years into the future. The first year of the plan is typically the annual budget and is expressed in substantial detail, the future years are less so.

**Capacity Planning** — The process of determining how much capacity will be required to produce in the future. Capacity planning can occur at an aggregate level (see **Resource Requirements Planning)** or at a detailed level.

**Collaborative Planning, Forecasting, and Replenishment (CPFR)** — A process involving participants in the supply chain centering on jointly managed planning and forecasting, with the goal of achieving very high efficiencies in replenishment. CPFR has been referred to as "second generation **Efficient Consumer Response.**"

**Demand Management** — The functions of sales forecasting, customer order entry, customer order promising, determining distribution center requirements, interplant orders, and service and supply item requirements. **Available-toPromise** and **Abnormal Demand** control play a large role in effective Demand Management.

**Demand Manager** — A job function charged with coordinating the **Demand Management** process. Frequently the Demand Manager will operate the statistical forecasting system and work closely with other marketing and salespeople in the Demand Planning phase of **Executive S&OP**. Other activities for the Demand Manager might include making decisions regarding **abnormal demand,** working closely with the Master Scheduler on product availability issues, and being a key player in other aspects of the monthly **Executive S&OP** process. This may or may not be a full-time position.

**Demand Plan** — The forecast, customer orders, and other anticipated demands such as interplant, export, and samples. See: **Sales Plan.**

**Demand/Supply Strategies** — A statement for each product family that defines how the company "meets the customer" with that product, its objectives in terms of customer service levels, and targets for finished inventory or order backlog levels. For example, Family A is Make-to-Stock (i.e., it is shipped to customers from finished goods inventory), its target line fill is 99.5 percent, and its target finished inventory level is ten days' supply.

**Design-to-Order** — An order fulfillment strategy that calls for detailed design of the product to begin after receipt of the customer order. This is frequently used in companies that make complex, highly-engineered, "one-of-a-kind" products. See: **Finish-to-Order, Make-to-Order, Make-to-Stock.**

**Detailed Forecast** — See: **Mix Forecast.**

**Enterprise Resource Planning (ERP)** — An enterprise-wide set of management tools with the ability to link customers and suppliers into a complete supply chain, employing proven business processes for decision-making, and providing for high degrees of cross-functional coordination among Sales, Marketing, Manufacturing, Operations, Logistics, Purchasing, Finance, New Product Development, and Human Resources.

**Exec Meeting** — The culminating step in the monthly **Executive S&OP** cycle. It is a decision-making meeting, attended by the president/general manager, his or her staff, and other key individuals.

**Executive S&OP** — The executive portion of the overall Sales & Operations Planning set of processes. Its mission is to balance demand and supply at the aggregate level and to align operational planning with financial planning. It is a cross-functional decision-making process involving the general manager of the business and his or her staff, along with managers and other support people. Executive S&OP includes the functions of **Demand Planning**, **Supply Planning**, the **Pre-Meeting**, and the **Executive Meeting**, occurring on a monthly cycle and displaying information in both units and dollars. Used properly, S&OP enables the company's managers to view the business holistically and provides them with a window into the future. See: **Sales & Operations Planning**.

**Family** — See: **Product Family.**

**Financial Interface**—A process of tying financial information and operating information together. It is the process by which businesses are able to operate with one and only one set of numbers, rather than using data in operational functions that differ from that used in the financial side of the business.

**Financial Planning** — The process of developing dollarized projections for revenues, costs, cash flow, other asset changes, and so forth.

**Finish-to-Order** — An order fulfillment strategy where the customer order is completed shortly after receipt. The key components used in the finishing or final assembly process are planned, and possibly stocked, based on sales forecasts. Receipt of a customer order initiates the finishing of the customized product. This strategy is useful where a large number of end products, most often due to a high degree of optionality within the product, can be finished quickly from available components. Syn: Assemble-to-Order, **Build-to-Order.**

**Forecast** — See: **Sales Forecast.**

**Forecast Error** — The amount that the forecast deviates from actual sales. Measures of forecast error include **Mean Absolute Deviation** (MAD) and **Sum of Deviations** (SOD). See: **Variability.**

**Forecast Horizon** — The amount of time into the future that the forecast covers.

**Lean Manufacturing** — A powerful approach to production that emphasizes the minimization of the amount of all the resources (including time) used in the various activities of the enterprise. It involves identifying and eliminating nonvalue-adding activities in design, production, **Supply Chain Management,** and customer relations.

**Make-to-Order** — An order fulfillment strategy where the product is made after receipt of a customer's order. The final product is usually a combination of standard items and items custom designed to meet the requirements called out in the customer order. See: **Design-to-Order, Finish-to-Order, Make-to-Stock.**

**Make-to-Stock** — An order fulfillment strategy where products are finished before receipt of customer orders. Customer orders are typically filled from existing finished goods inventory. See: **Design-to-Order, Finish-to-Order, Make-toOrder.**

**Manufacturing Resource Planning (MRP II)** — See: **Enterprise Resource Planning.**

**Master Schedule** — The tool that balances demand and supply at the product level, as opposed to **Executive S&OP,** which balances demand and supply at the aggregated **Product Family** level. It is the source of customer order promising, via its **Available-to-Promise** capability, and contains the anticipated build schedule for the plant(s) in the form of the **Master Production Schedule.**

**Mix** — The details: individual products, customer orders, pieces of equipment, as opposed to aggregate groupings. See: **Volume.**

**Mix Forecast** — A forecast by individual products. Sometimes called the detailed forecast. It is used for short-term scheduling for plants and suppliers (and may be required for certain long lead time, unique purchased items).

**Operations Plan** — The agreed-upon rates and volumes of production or procurement to support the **Sales Plan (Demand Plan, Sales Forecast)** and to reach the inventory or order backlog targets. The Operations Plan, upon authorization at the **Executive Meeting,** becomes the "marching orders" for the Master Scheduler, who must set the **Master Production Schedule** in congruence with the Operations Plan. Syn: **Production Plan.**

**Pre-Meeting** — The preliminary session prior to the **Executive Meeting.** In it, key people from Sales & Marketing, Operations, Finance, and New Product Development come together to develop the recommendations to be made at the Executive S&OP session.

**Product Family** — The basic planning element for **Executive S&OP,** where the focus is on families and subfamilies (volume), not individual items (mix).

**Product Subfamily** — A planning element sometimes used in **Executive S&OP** that provides a more detailed view than product families, but not at the extreme detail of individual products. Product Family A, for example, might contain three subfamilies — A1, A2, A3 — and each of those might contain a dozen or so individual products. See: **Product Family.**

**Production Plan** — See: **Operations Plan.**

**Resource** — Those things that add value to products in their production and/or delivery.

**Resource Requirements Planning** — The process by which the **Operations Plan** in **Executive S&OP** can be converted into future capacity requirements. Frequently the Operations Plan, expressed in units of product, is "translated" into standard hours of workload (which is a common unit of measure for production operations). Resource Requirements Planning can be used at the departmental level, or for subsets of departments, down to individual pieces of equipment or specific skill levels for production associates. This process can also be carried out for material requirements from suppliers, for warehouse space, and for non-production operations such as product design and drafting. A similar process, called **Rough-Cut Capacity Planning**, operates at the mix level in conjunction with the **Master Schedule**.

**Rough-Cut Capacity Planning**. Often used as a synonym for **Resource Requirements Planning.** In a more technical sense, Rough-Cut Capacity Planning refers to capacity requirements generated from the Master Schedule (mix), while Resource Requirements Planning indicates the requirements came from the Operations Plan (volume),

**Sales & Operations Planning (S&OP)** —A set of business processes – **Executive S&OP, Master Scheduling, Distribution Planning, Plant** and **Supplier Scheduling** and so forth – that helps companies keep demand and supply in balance., align units and dollars, and link volume planning with detailed mix schedules and plans. It does that by first focusing on aggregate volumes — product families and groups — so that mix issues — individual products and customer orders — can be handled more readily. The **Executive S&OP** component of Sales & Operations Planning links the company's Strategic Plans and **Business Plan** to its detailed processes — the order entry, **Master**

**Sales Forecast** — A projection of estimated future demand.

**Sales Plan** — The details backing up the **Sales Forecast.** It represents Sales & Marketing management's commitment to take all reasonable steps necessary to achieve the forecasted level of actual customer orders.

**Stockkeeping Unit (SKU)** — An individual finished product. In the more rigorous use of the term, it refers to a specific, individual product in a given location. Thus, product #1234 at the Los Angeles warehouse is a different SKU from the same product at the Chicago warehouse.

**Subfamily** — See: **Product Subfamily.**

**Supplier Scheduling** — A purchasing approach that provides suppliers with schedules rather than individual hard copy purchase orders. Normally a supplier scheduling system will include a contract and a daily or weekly schedule for each participating supplier extending for some time into the future. Syn: vendor scheduling.

**Supply Chain** — The organizations and processes involved from the initial raw materials through manufacturing and distribution to the ultimate acquisition of the finished product by the end consumer.

**Supply Chain Management** — The planning, organizing, and controlling of supply chain activities.

**Supply Planning** — The function of setting planned rates of production (both in-house and outsourced) to satisfy the **Demand Plan** and to meet inventory and order backlog targets. Frequently, **Resource Requirements Planning** is used to support this.

**Unaligned Resources** — Resources that do not match up with the product families. For example, Department 1 makes products in Families A, C, D, and G. Determining future capacity requirements for matrix resources is somewhat more complex than for aligned resources. Syn: Matrix Resources. See: **Aligned Resources.**

**Volume** — The big picture: sales and production rates for aggregate groupings — product families, production departments, etc. — as opposed to individual products, customer orders, and work centers. See: **Mix.**

**Volume Forecast** — A forecast by product groupings such as families, classes, and so forth. Also called the aggregate forecast or the product group forecast, it is used for sales planning, for **Capacity Planning** at the plants and suppliers, and for financial analysis and planning.

# Index